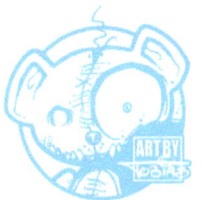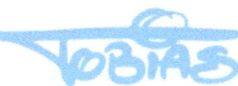

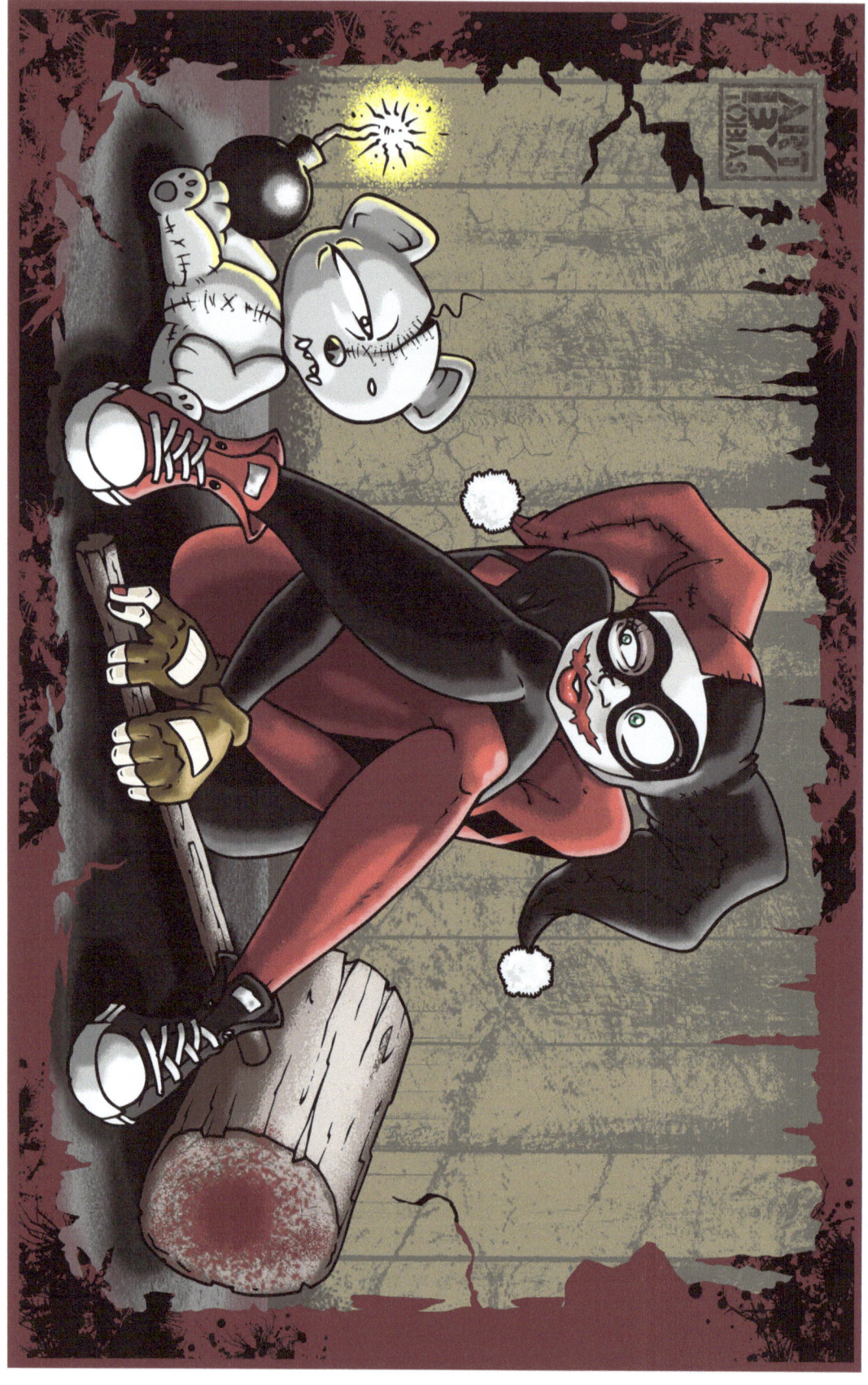

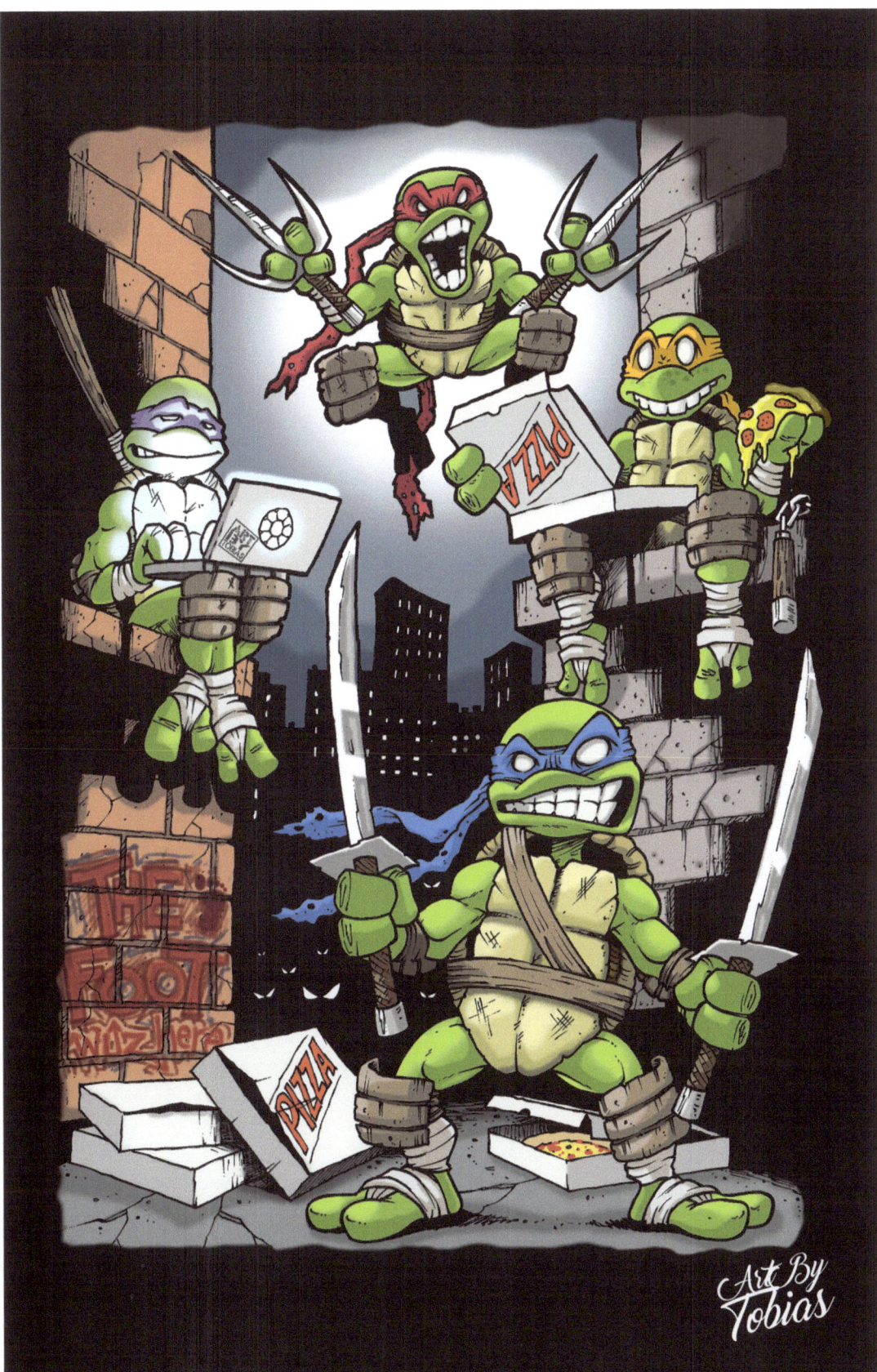

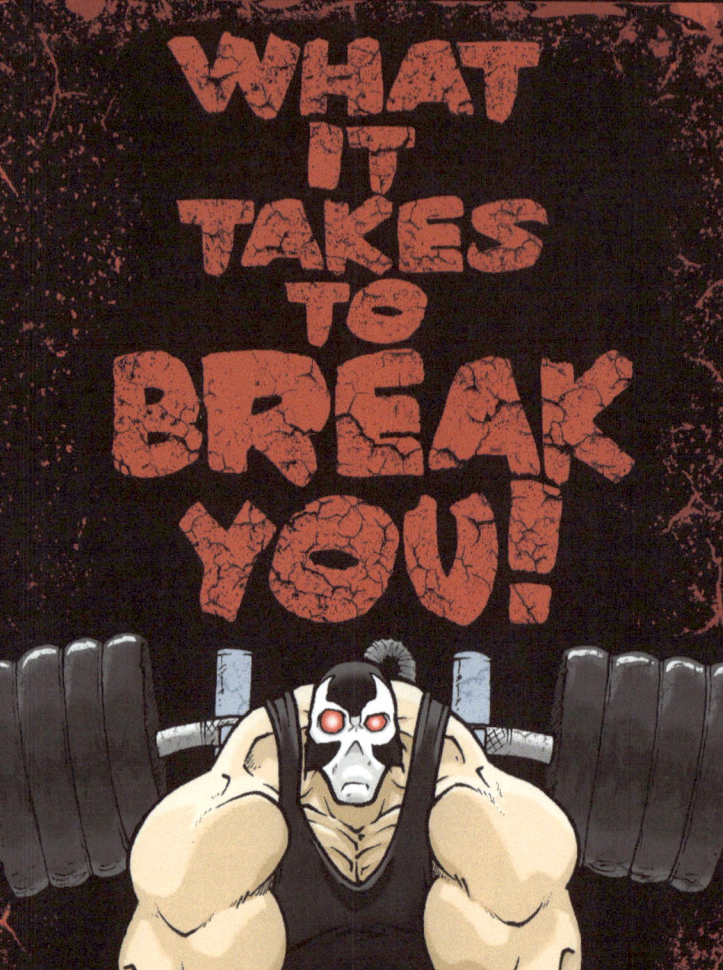

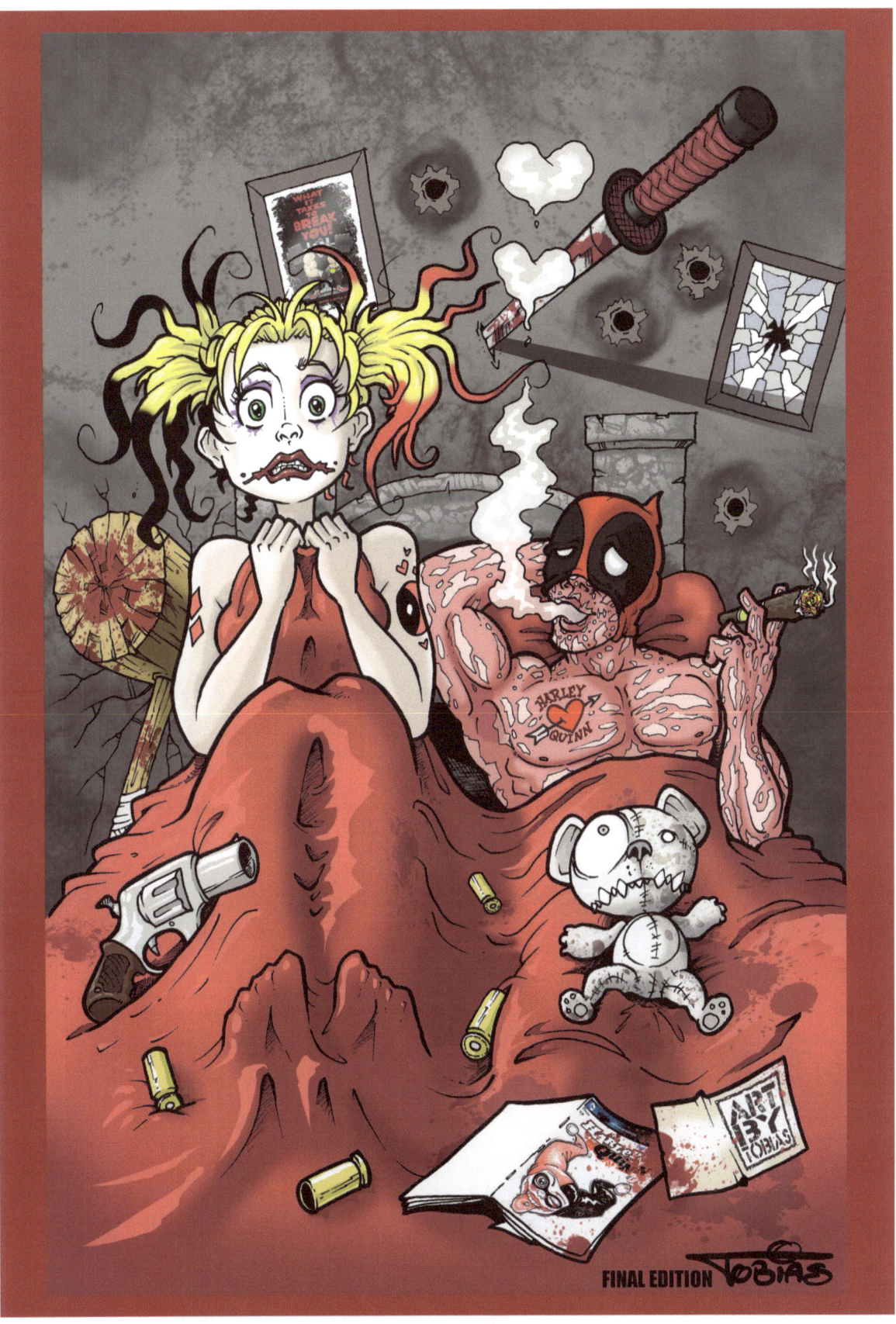

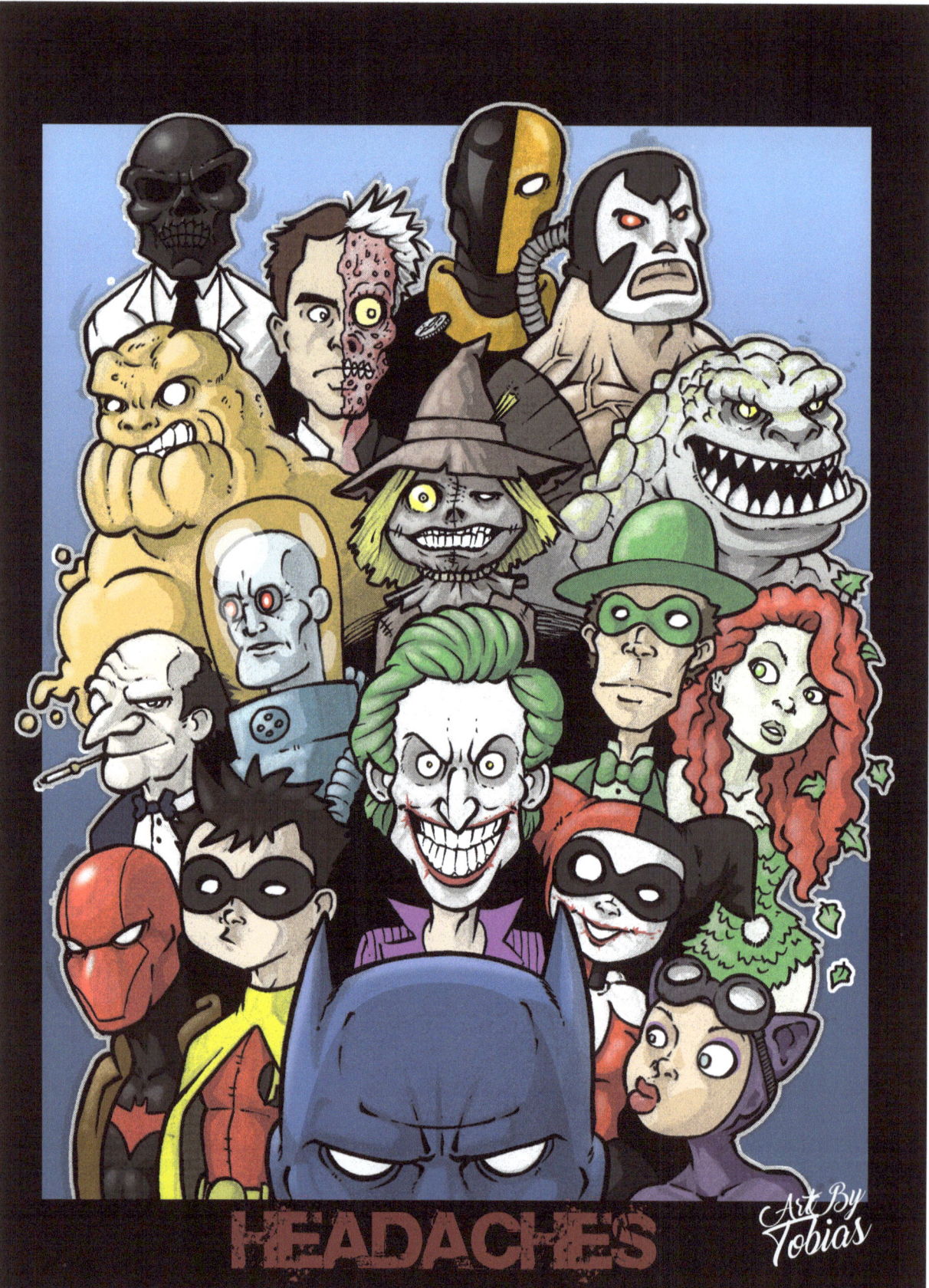

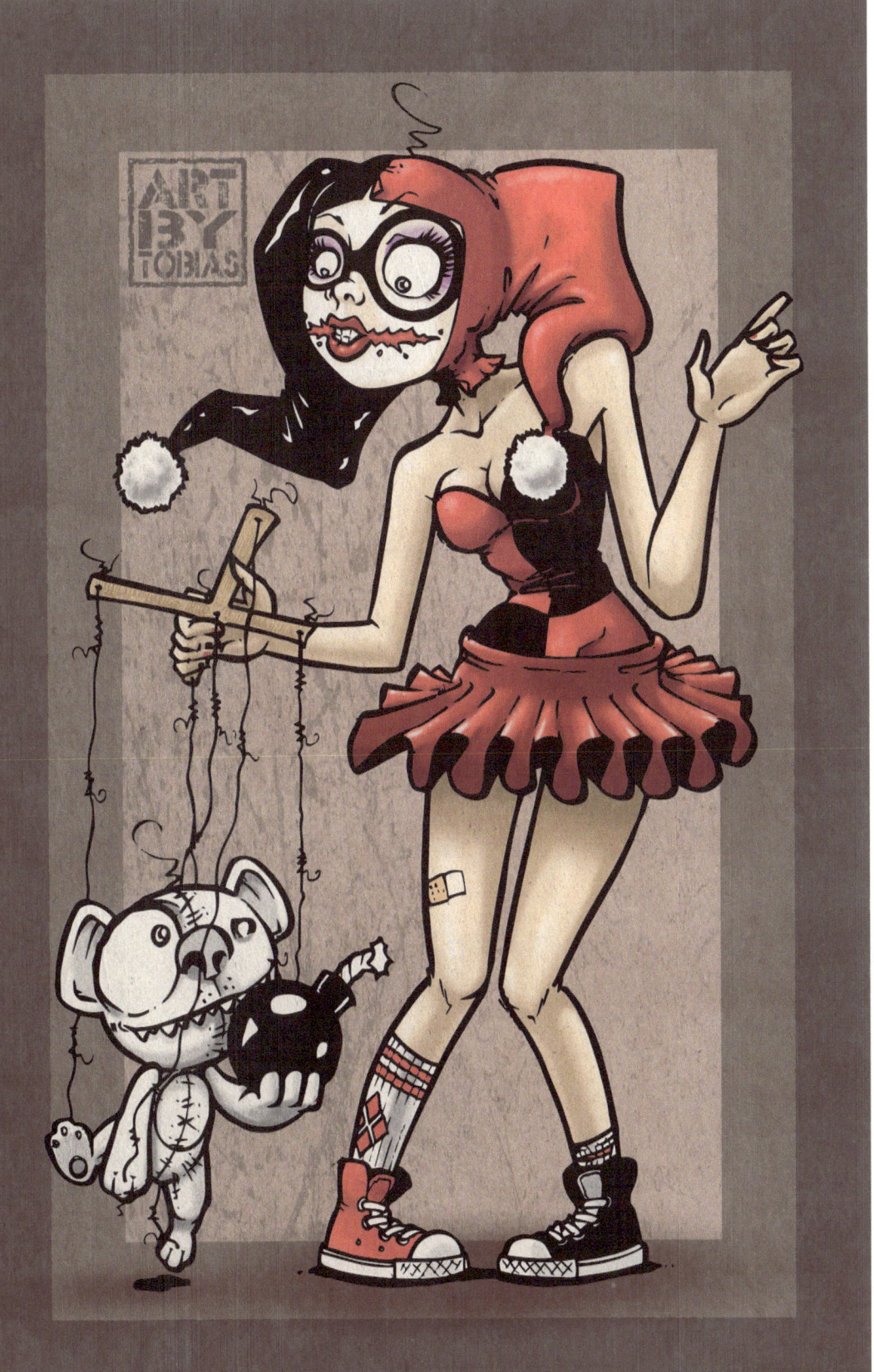

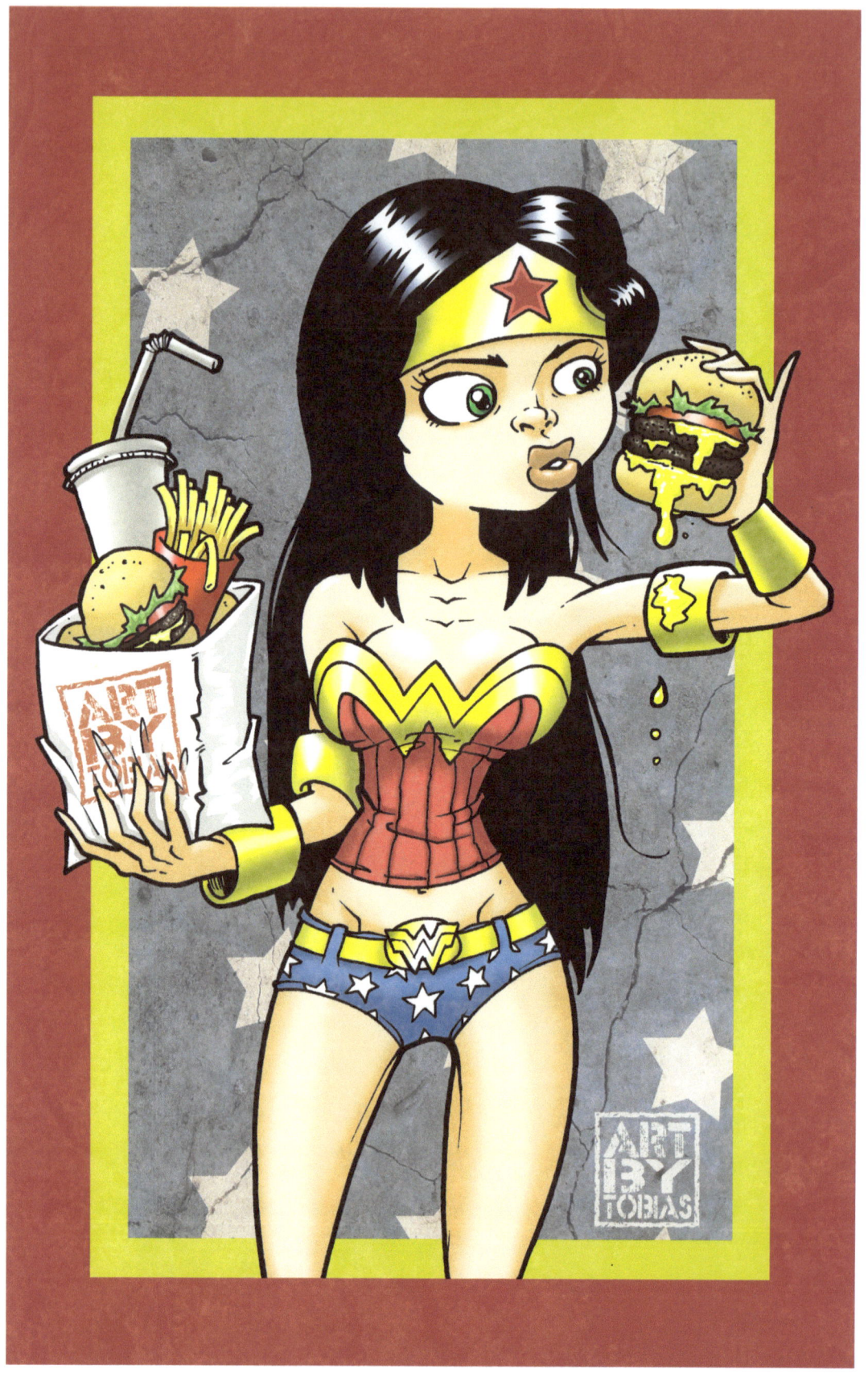

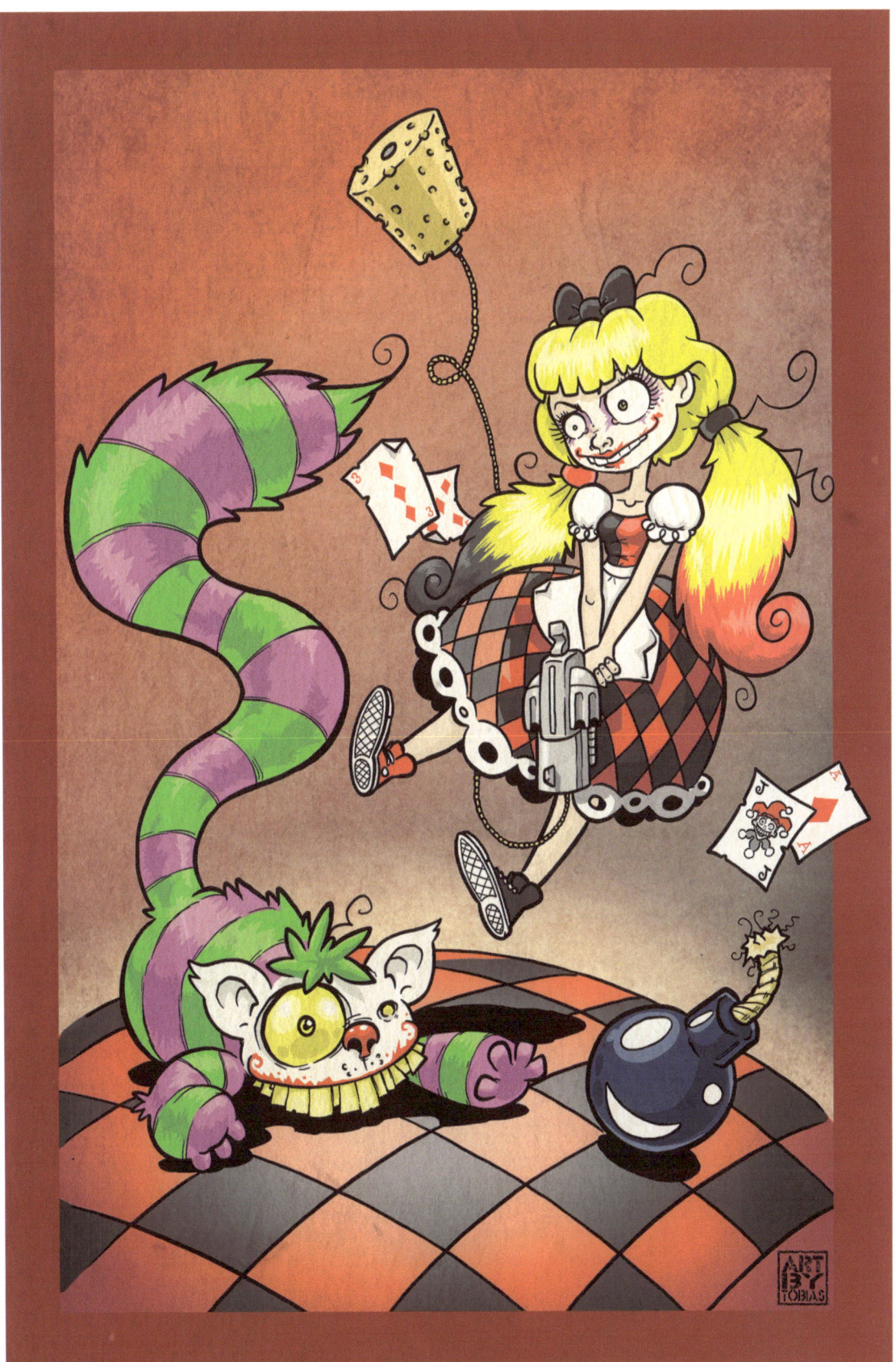

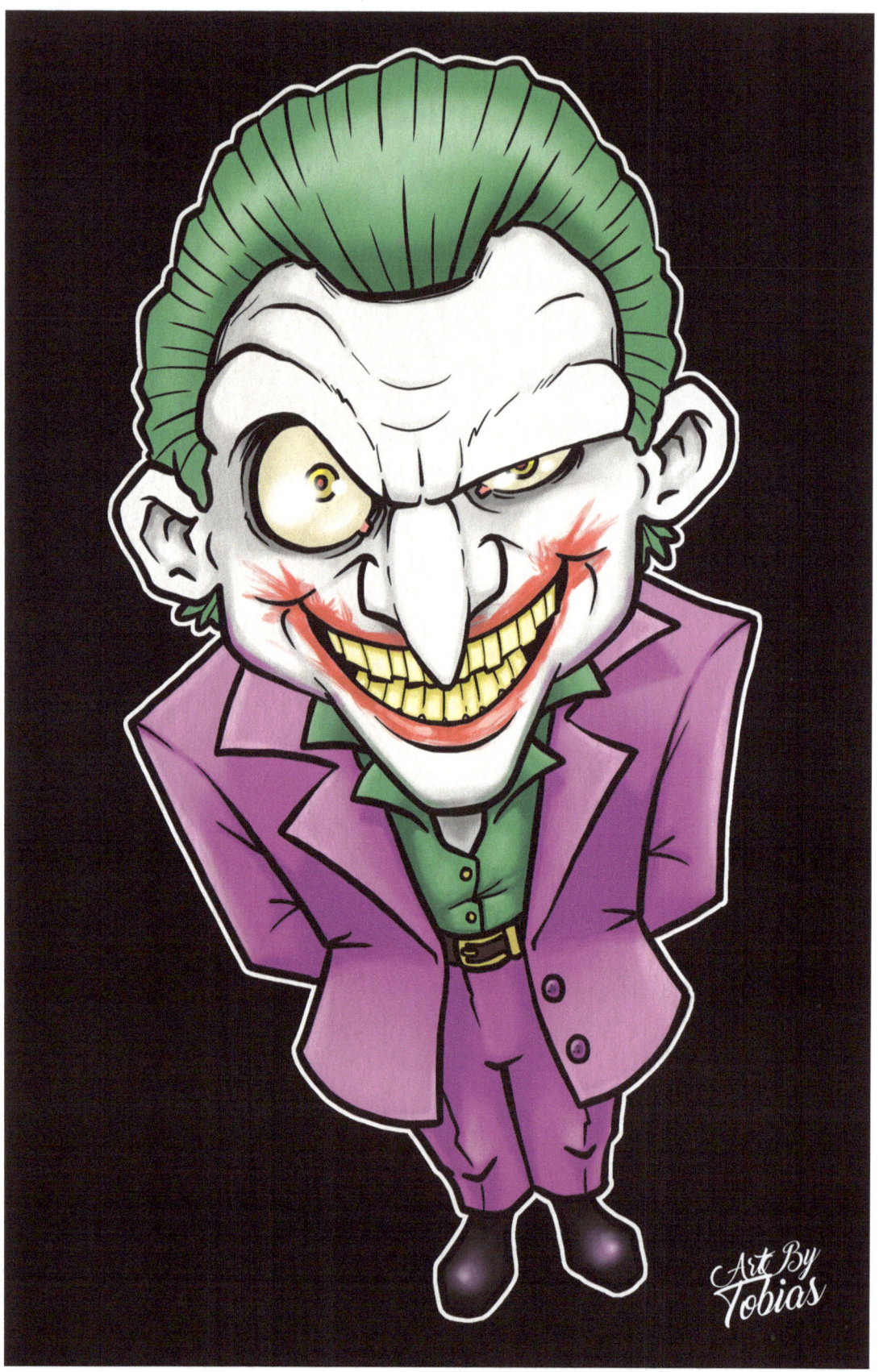

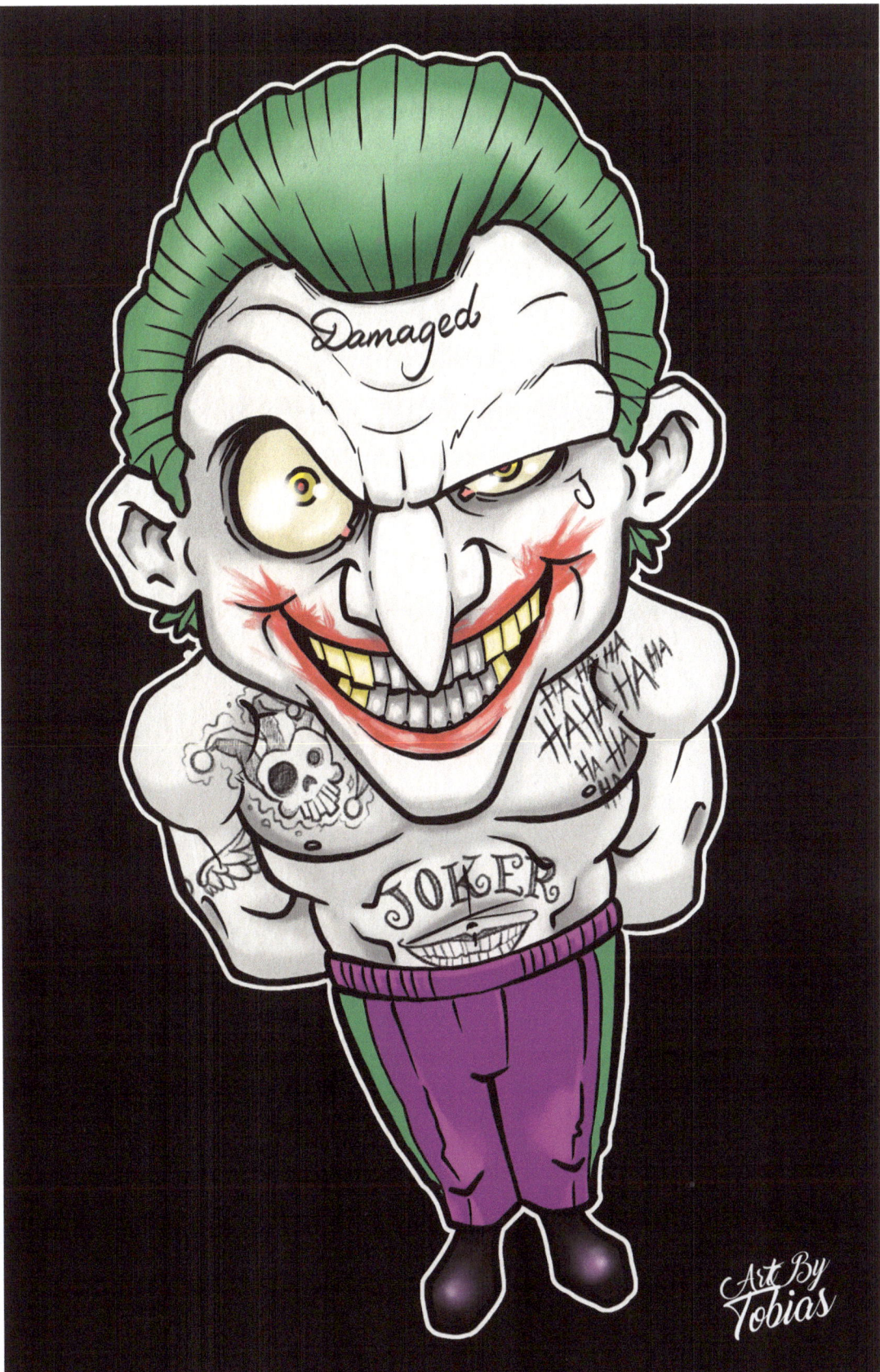

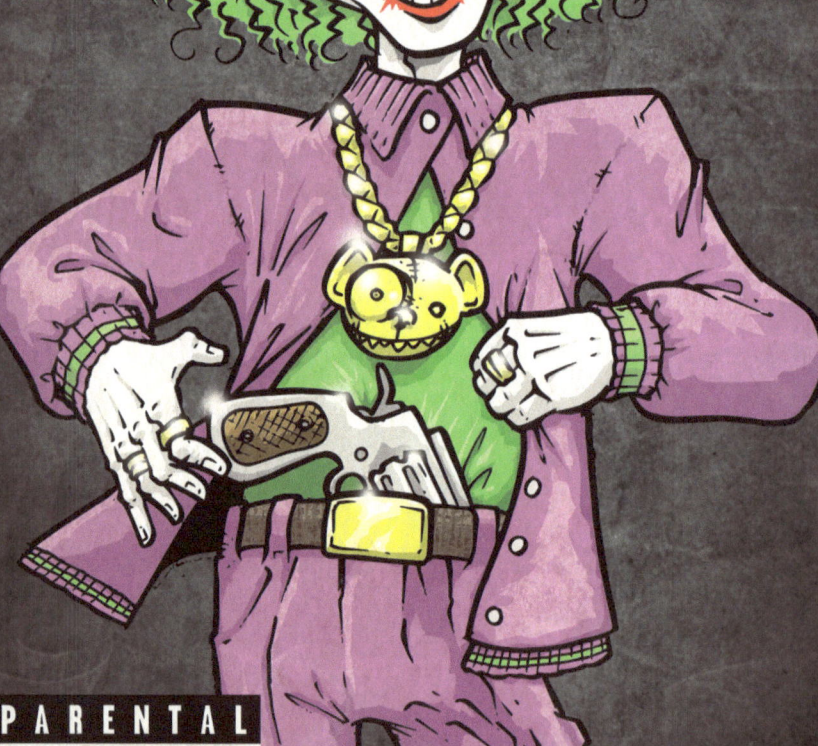

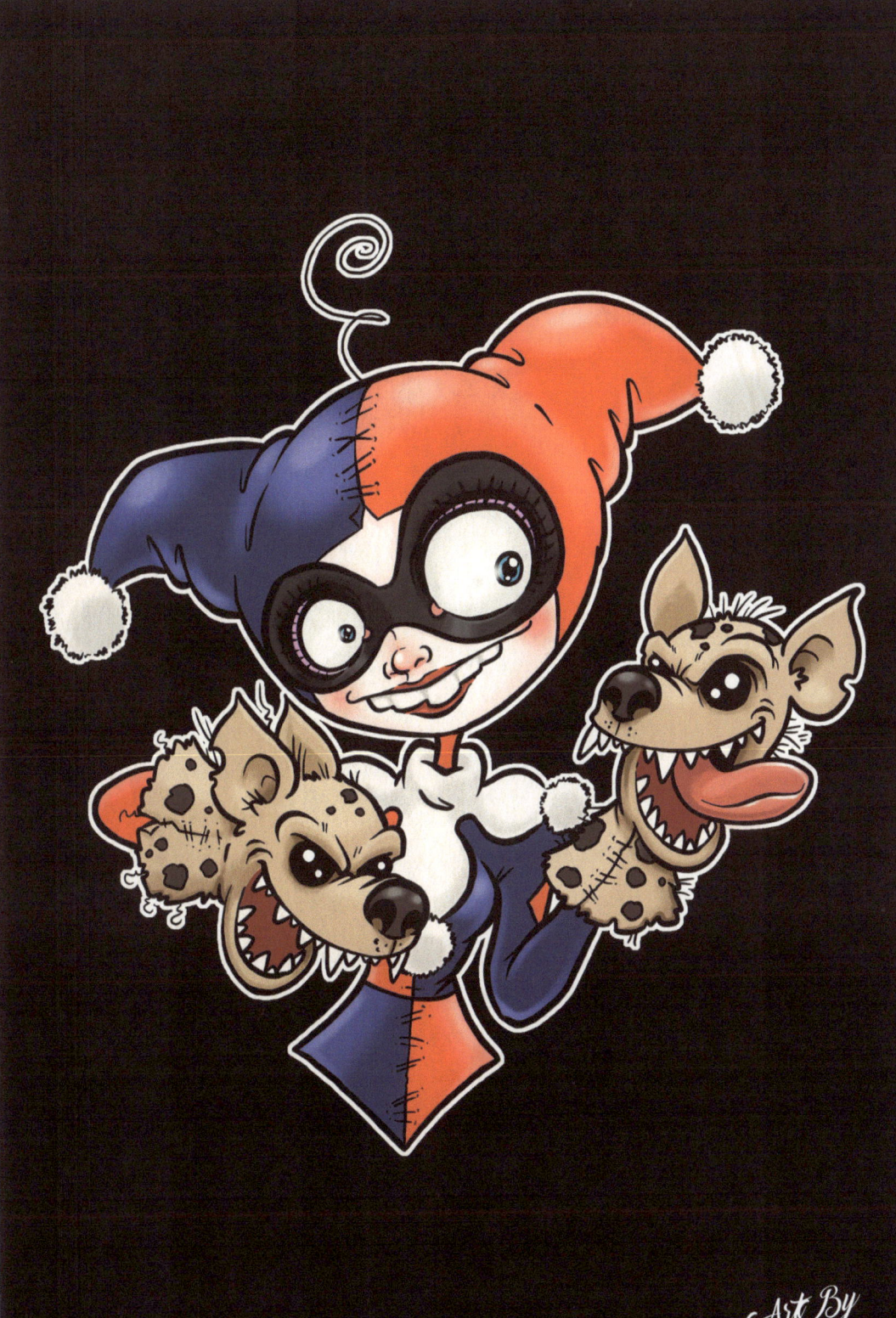

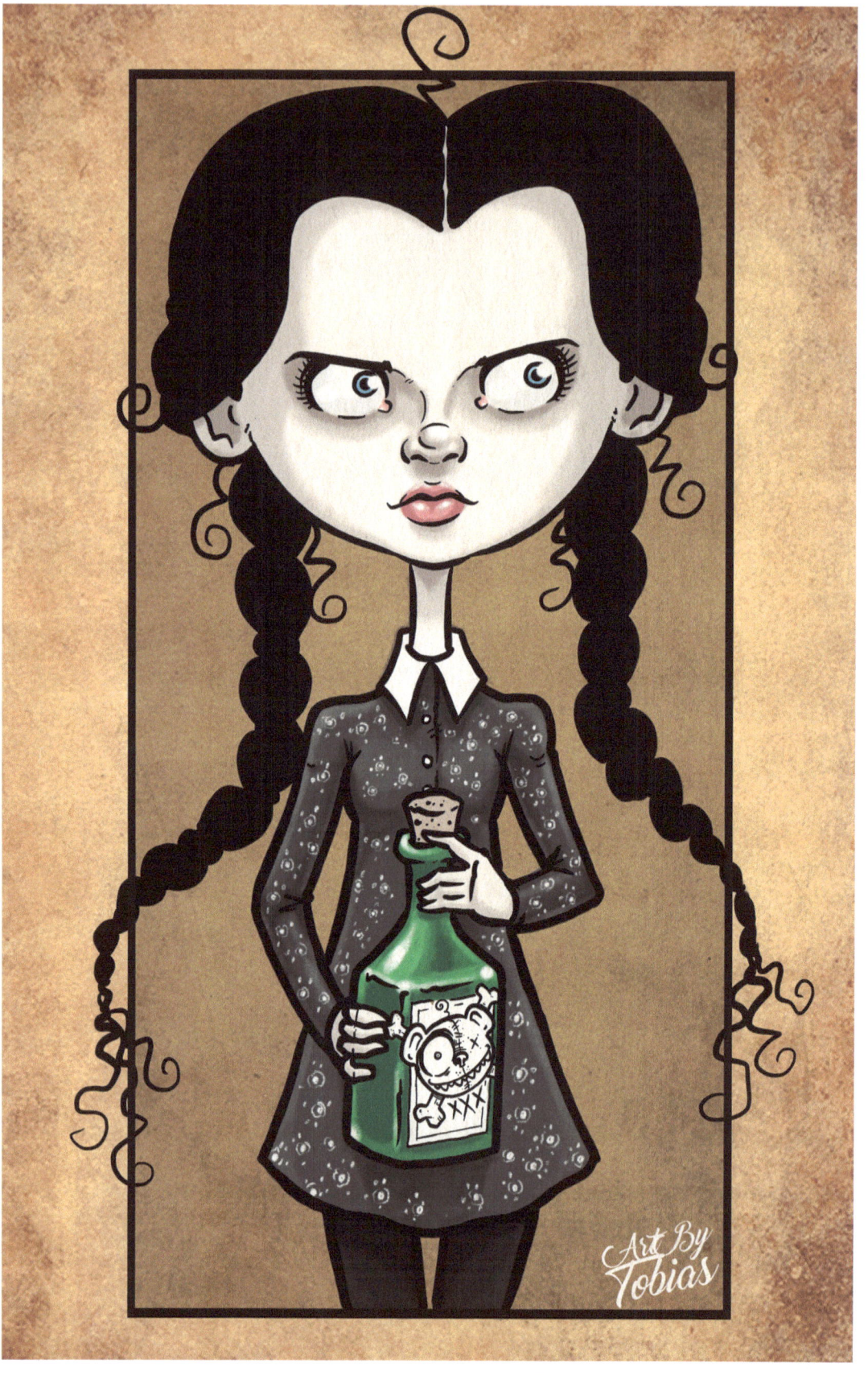

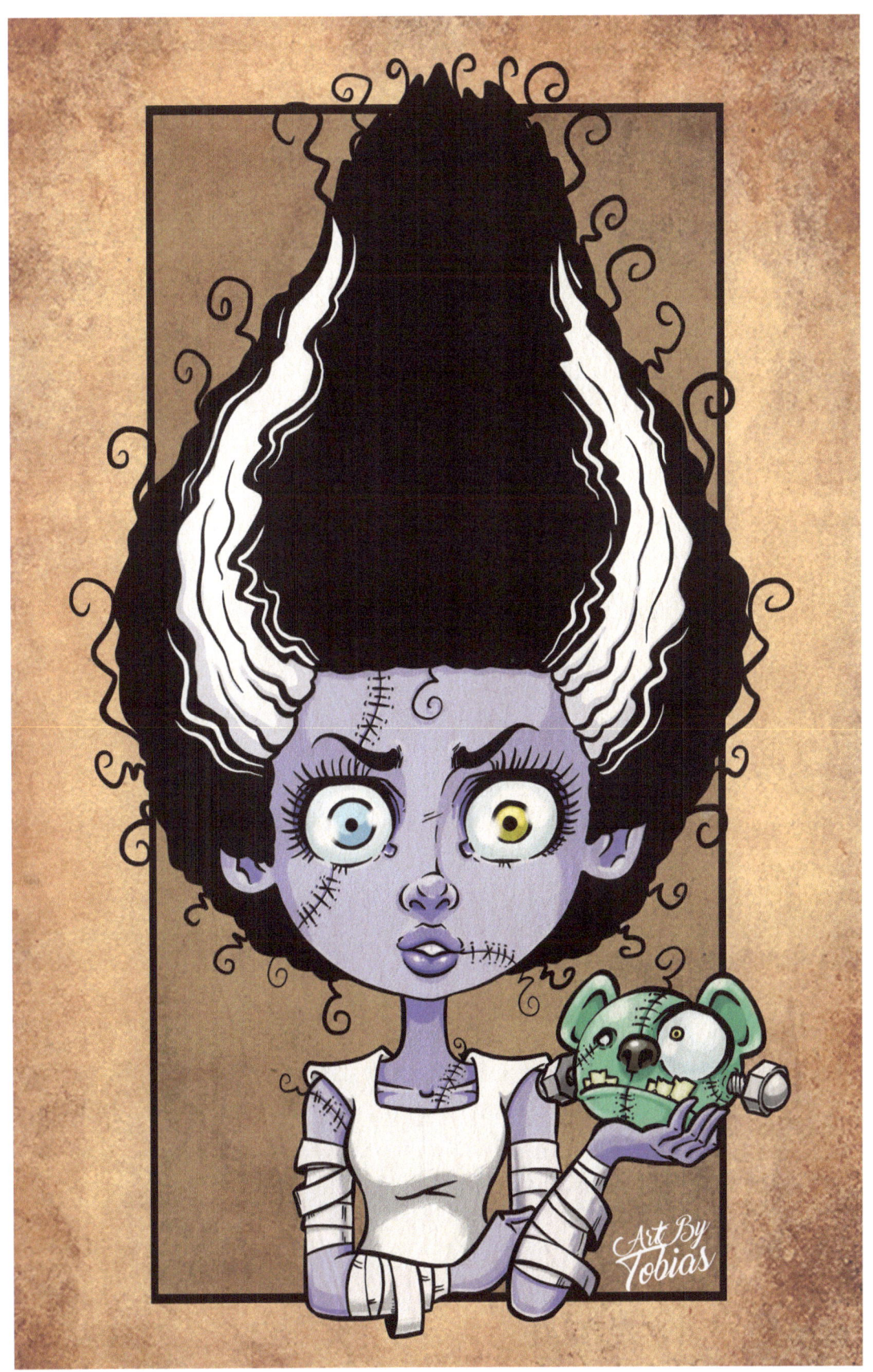

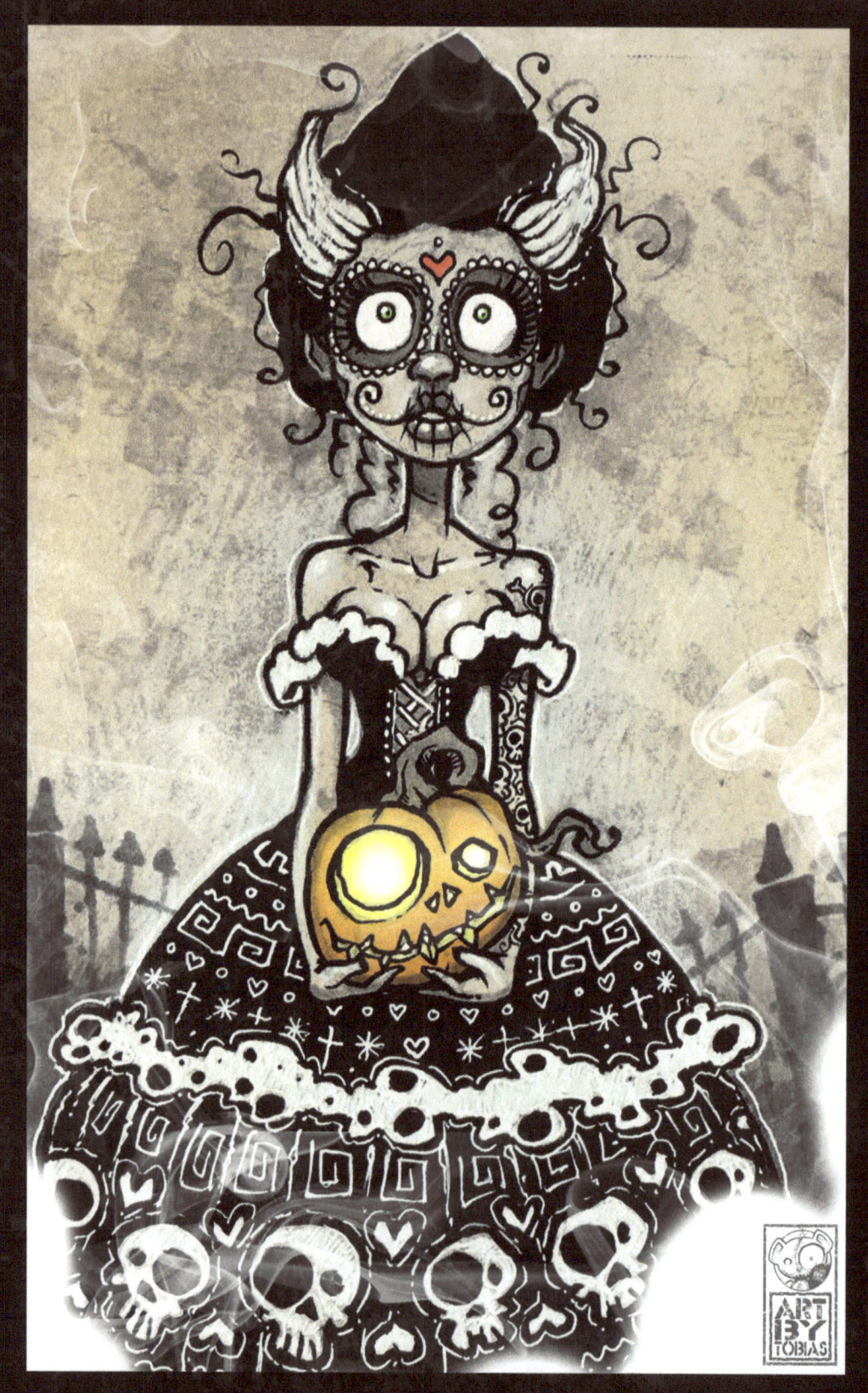

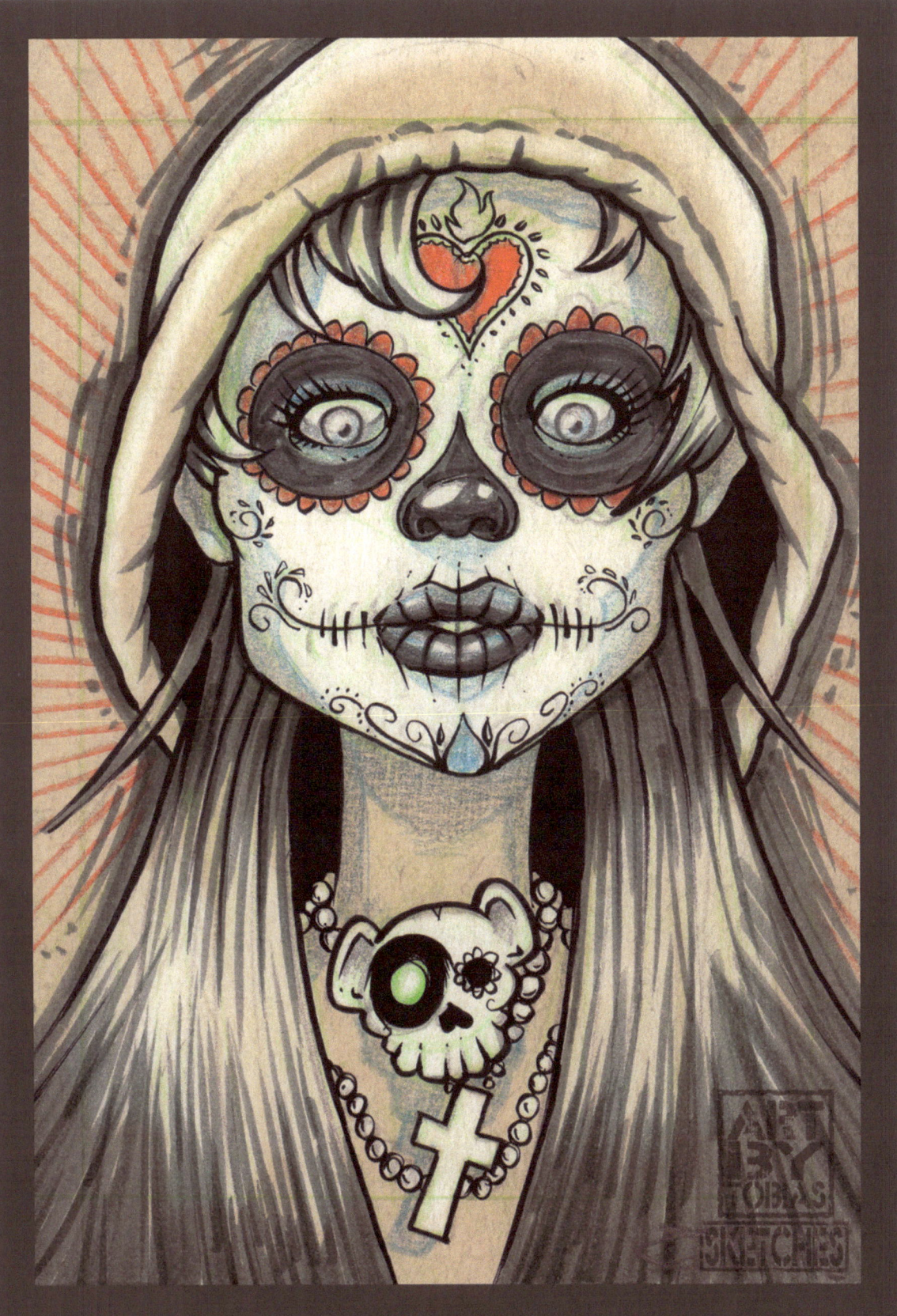

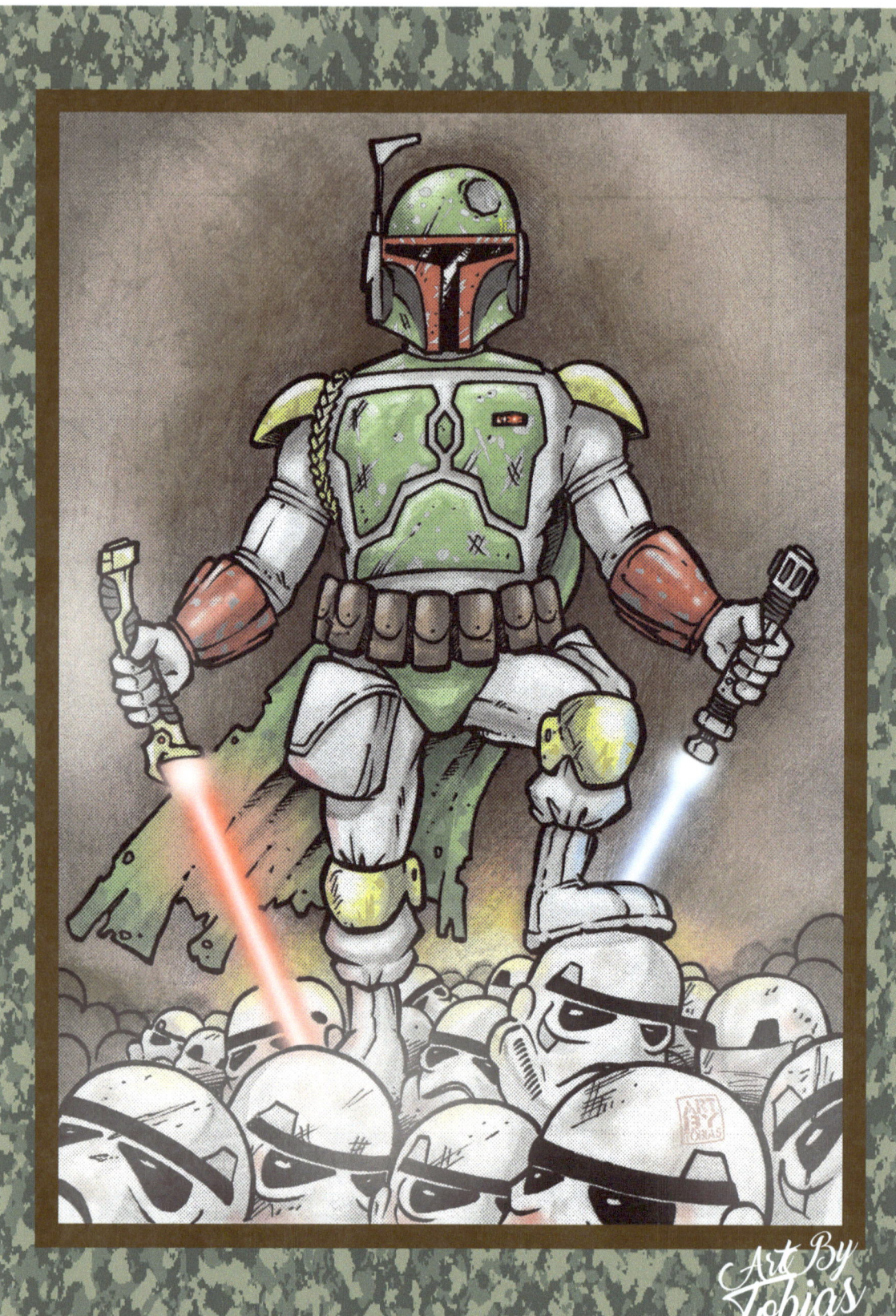

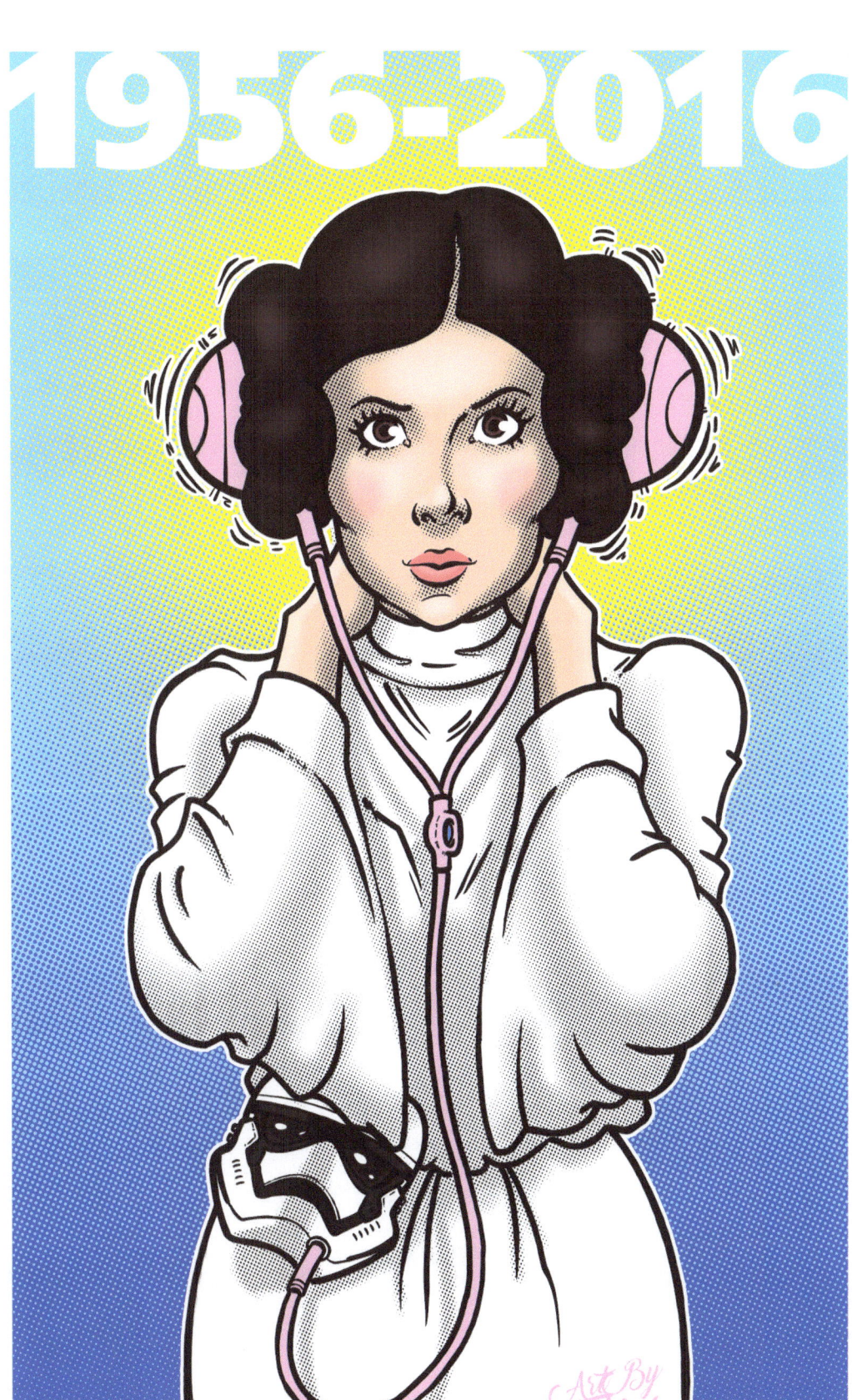

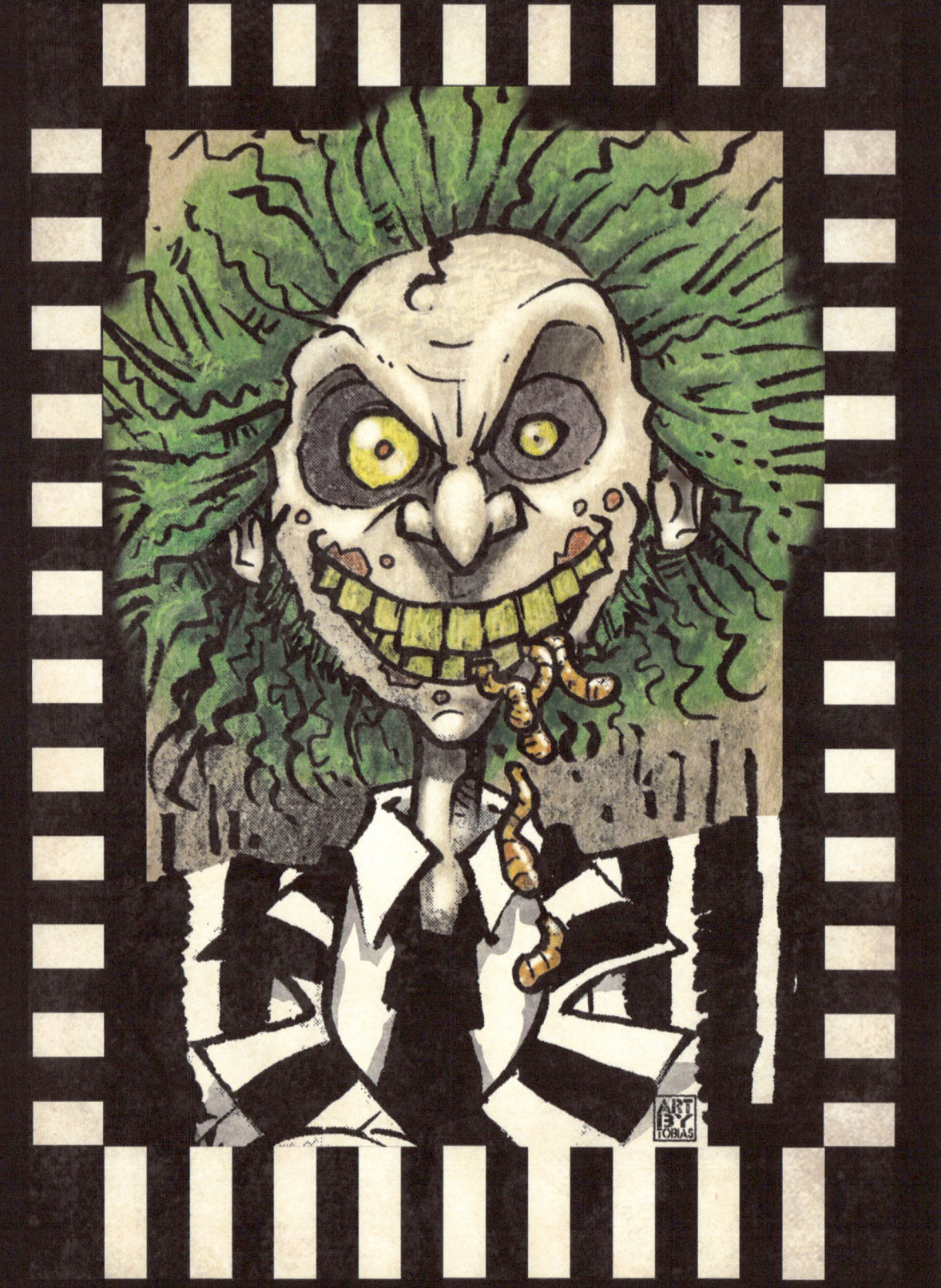

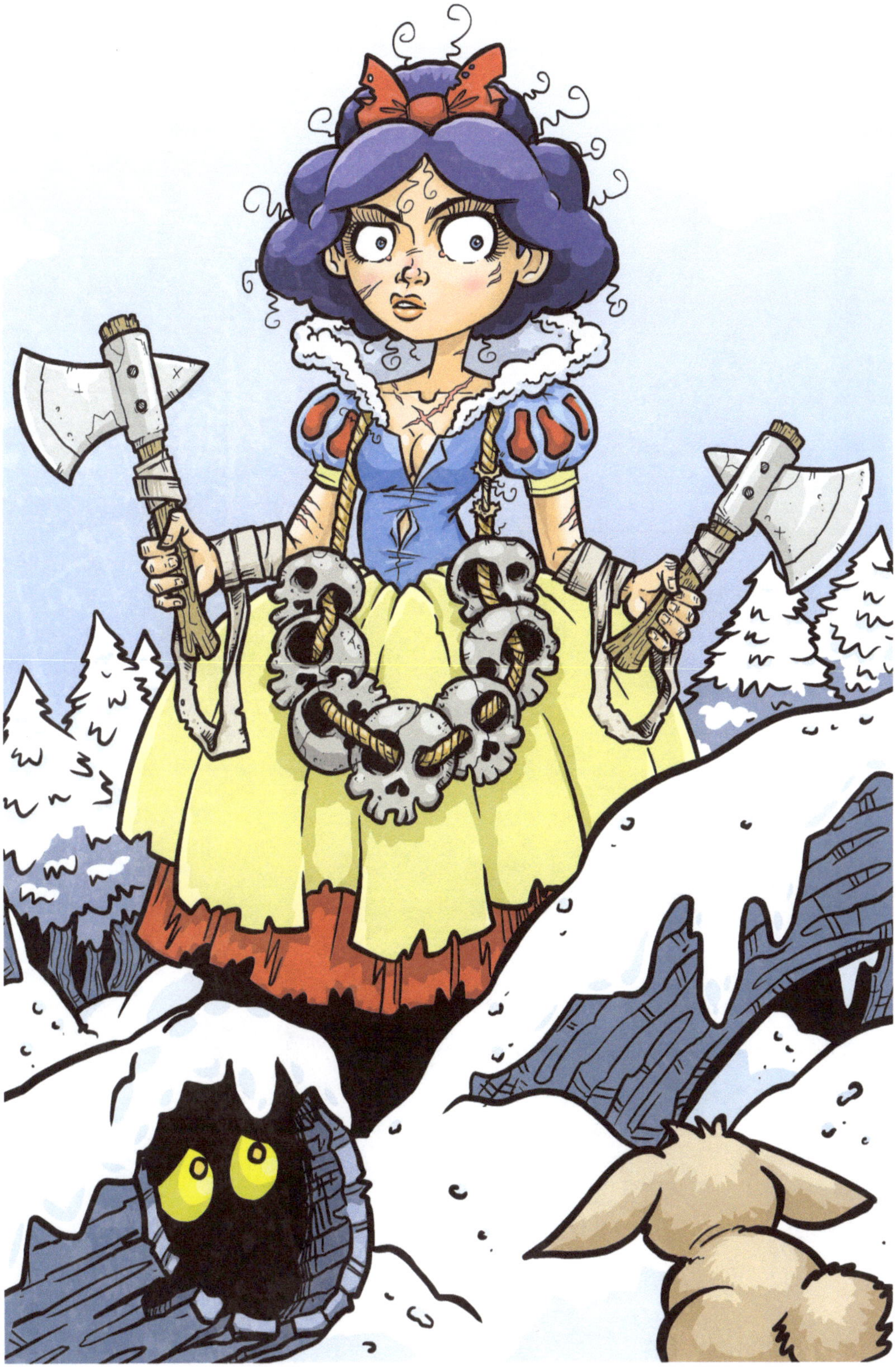

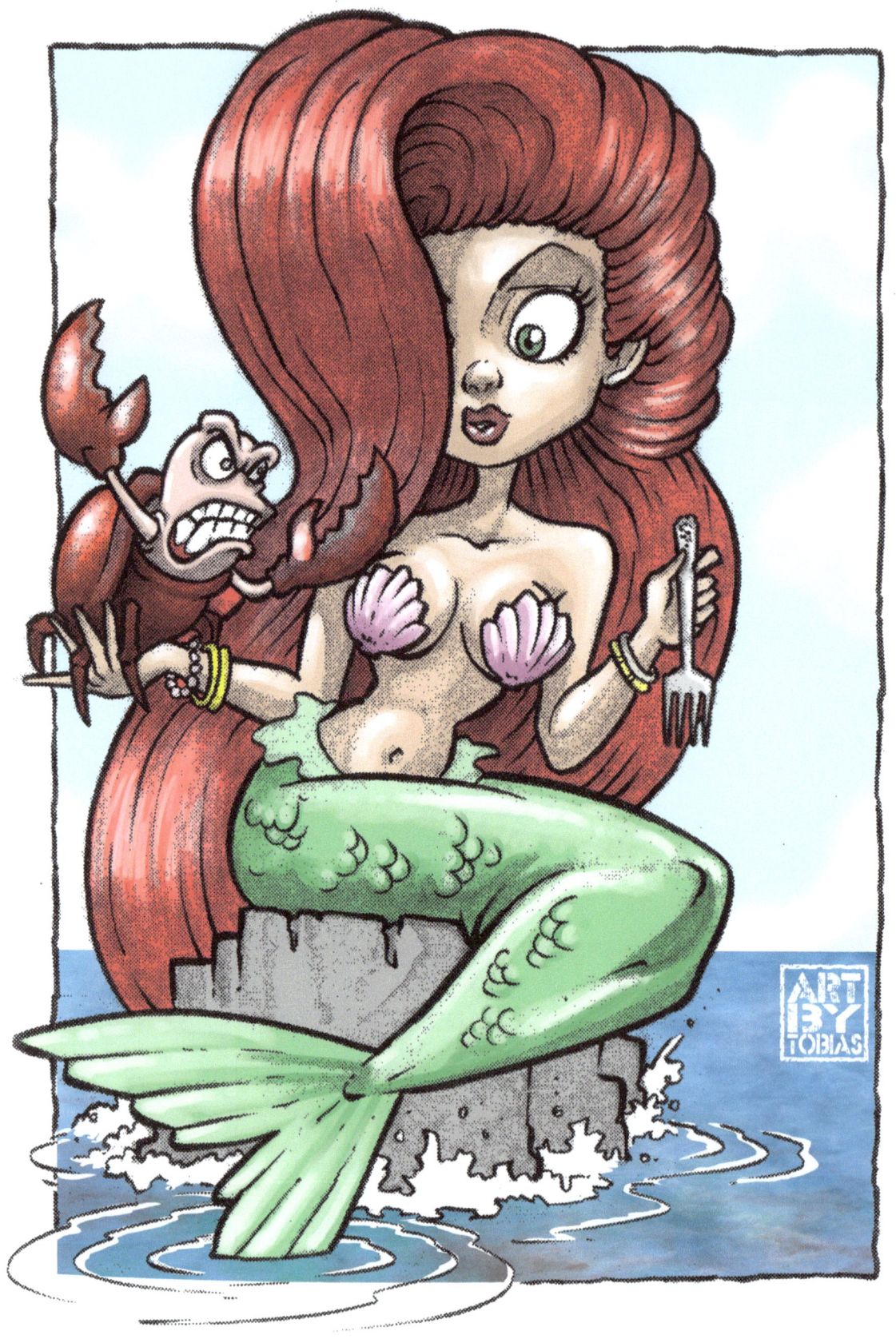

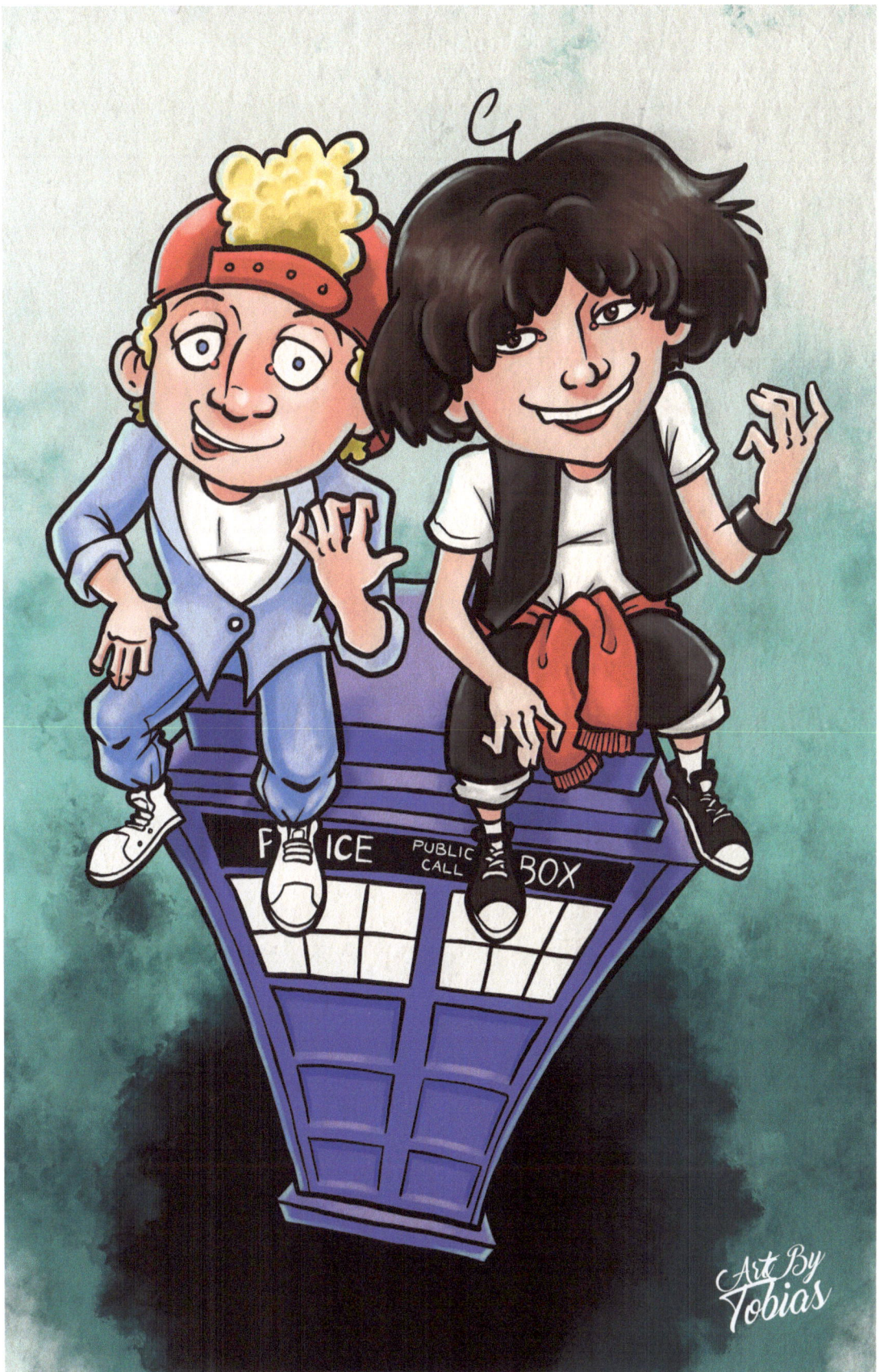

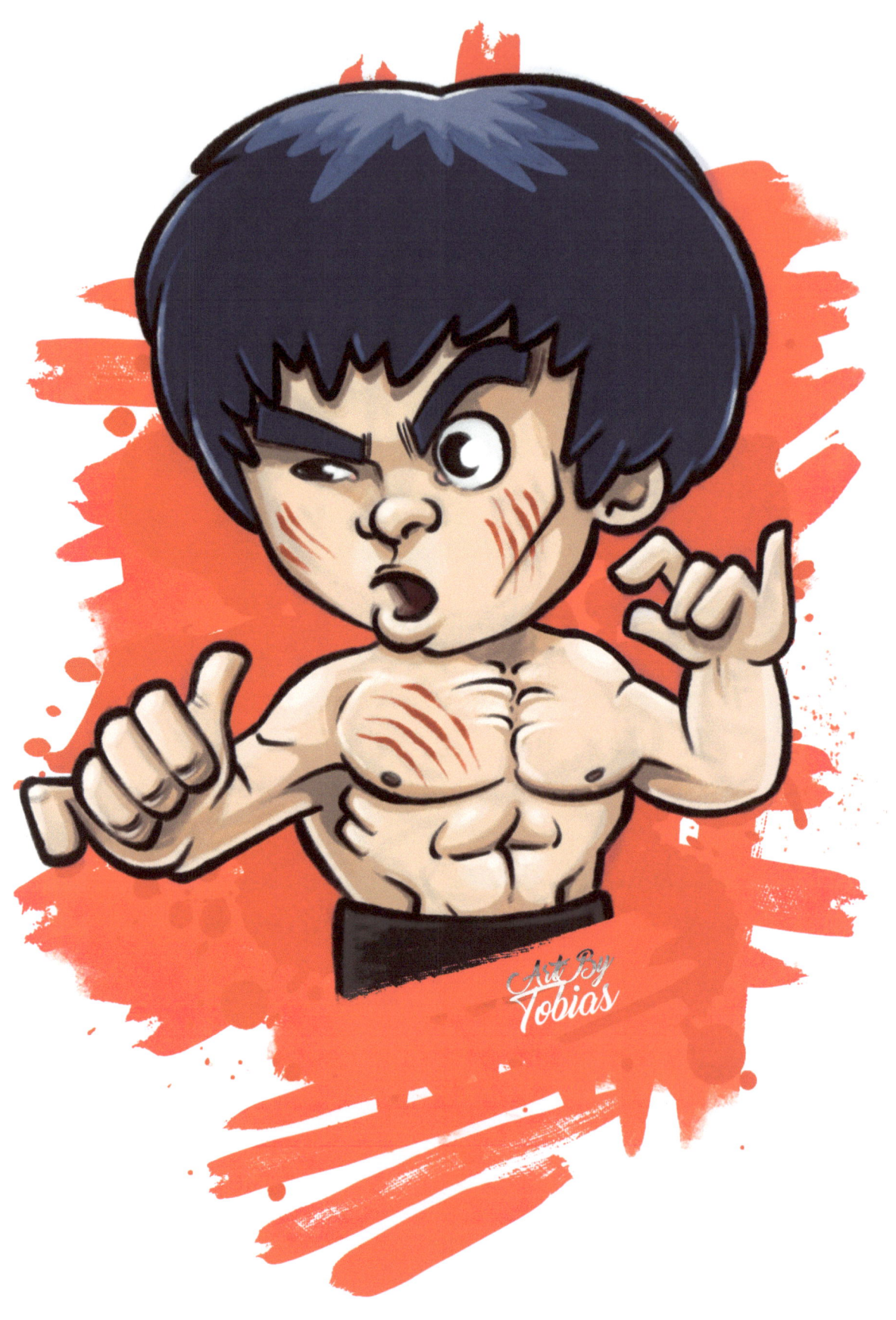

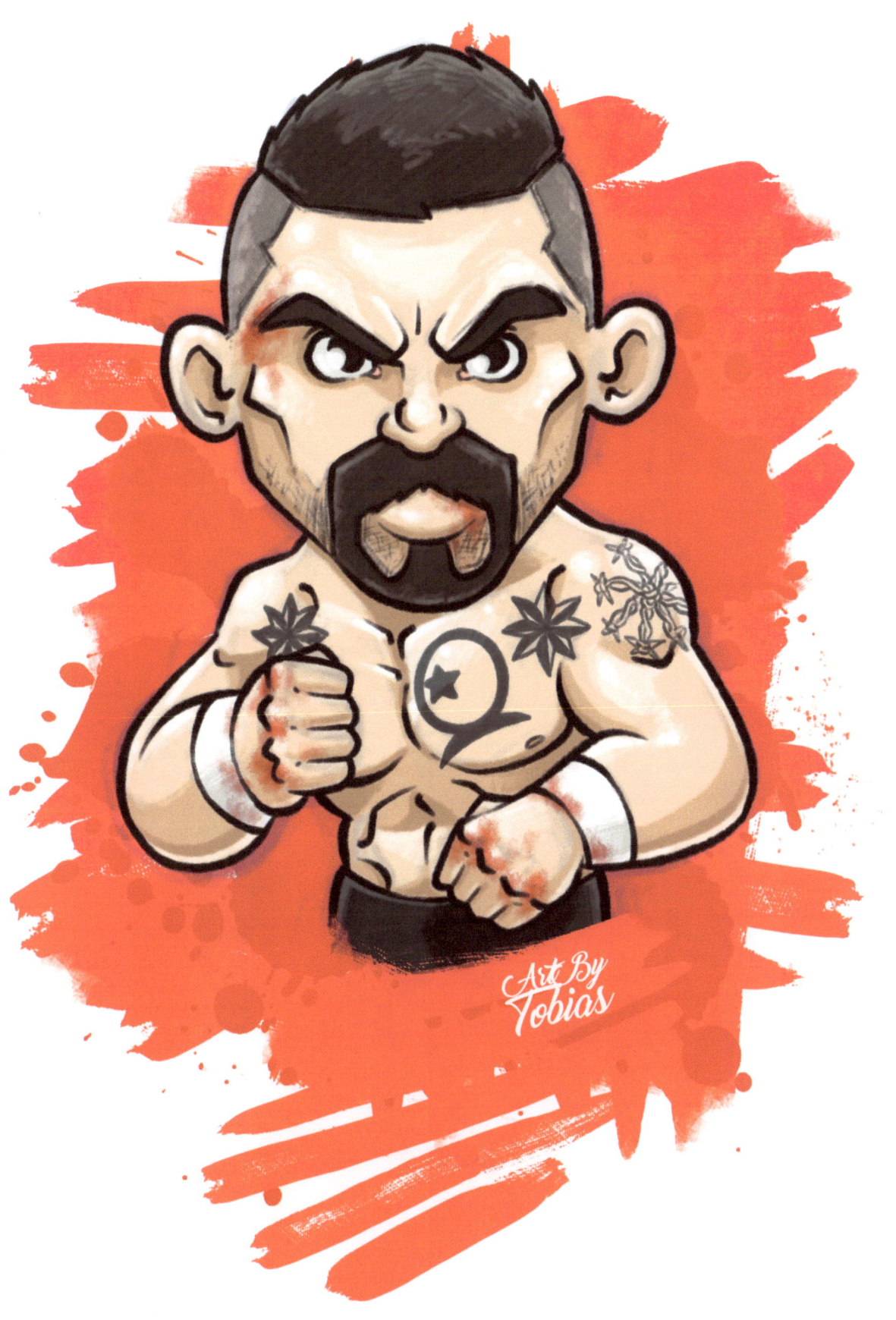

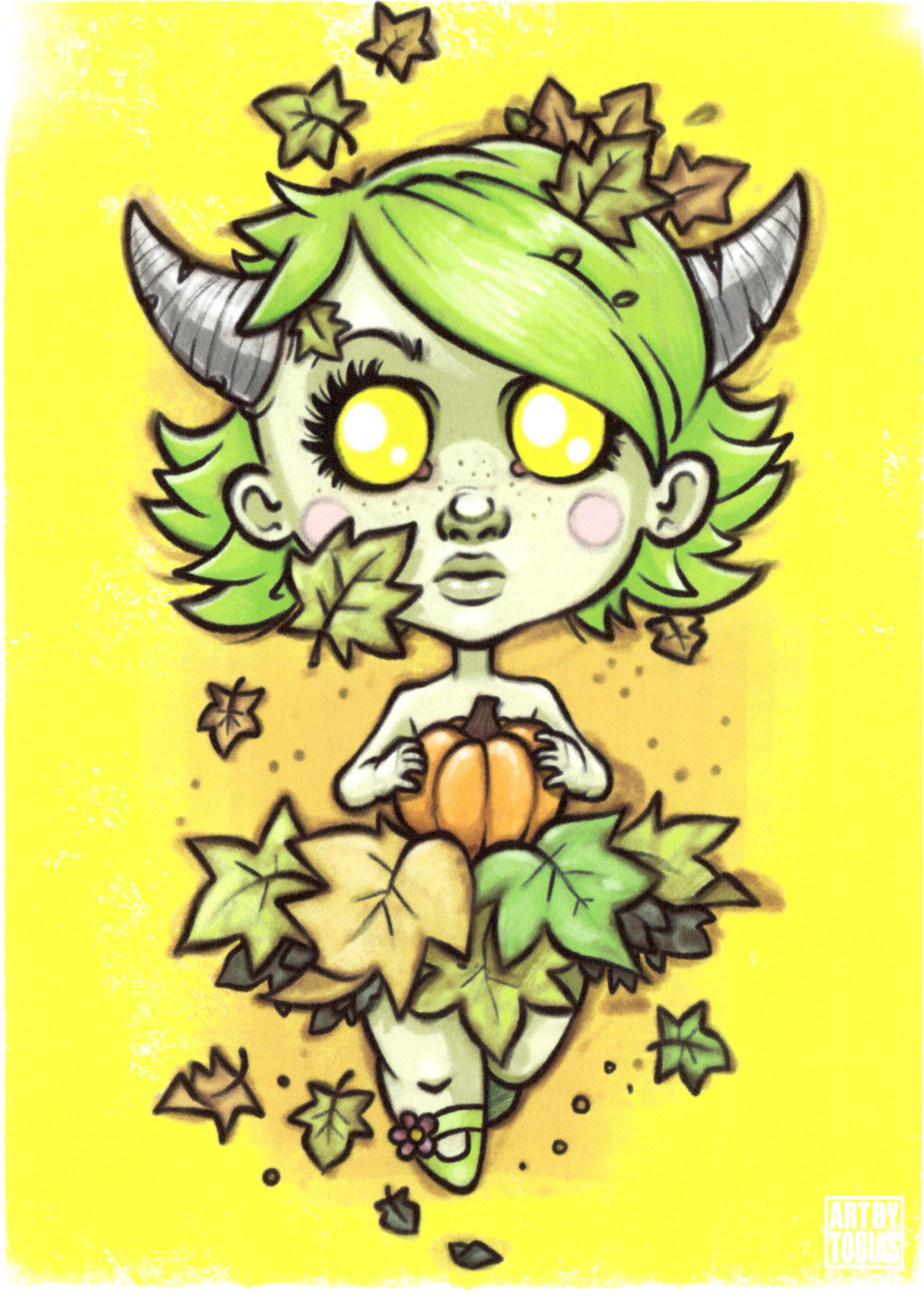

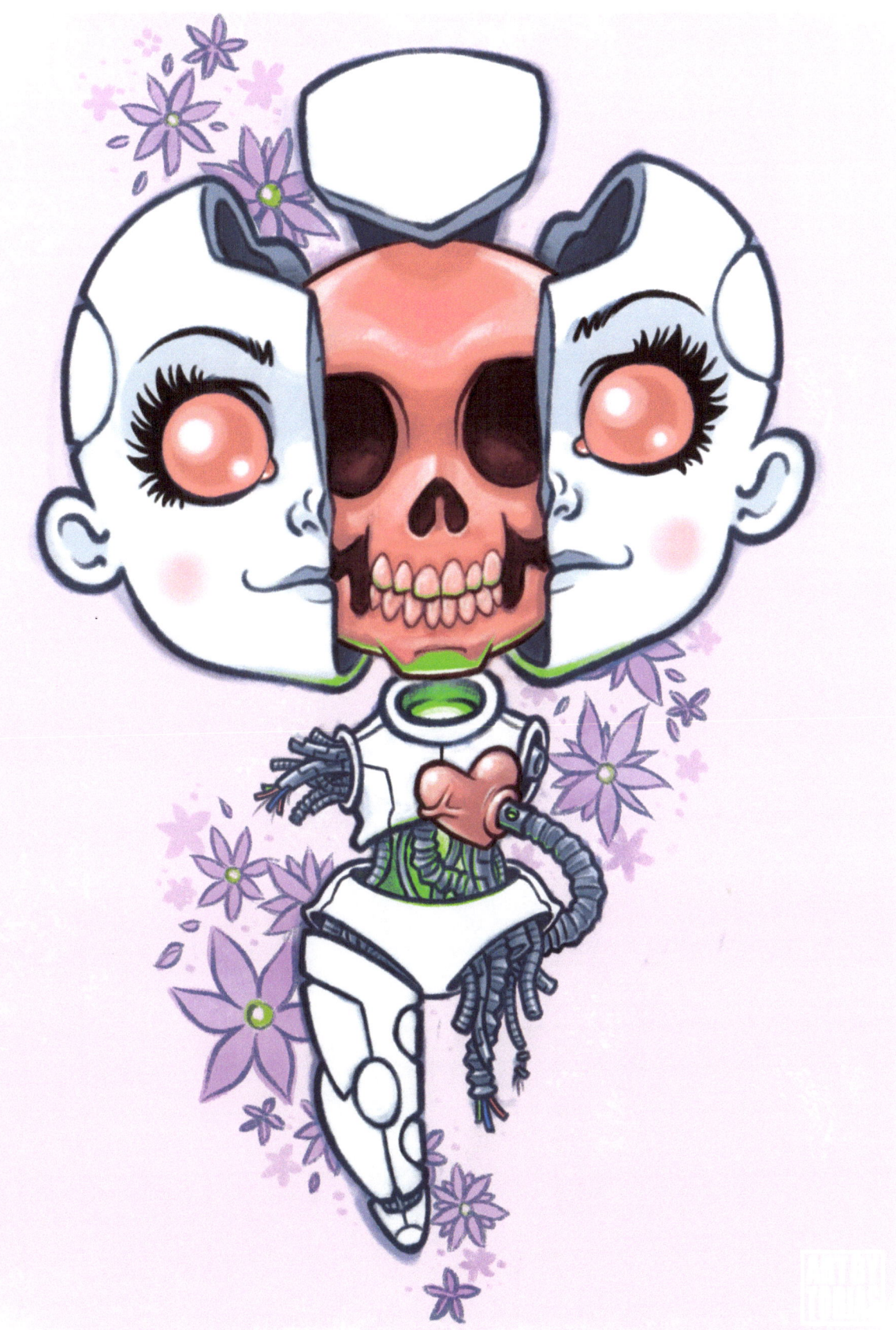

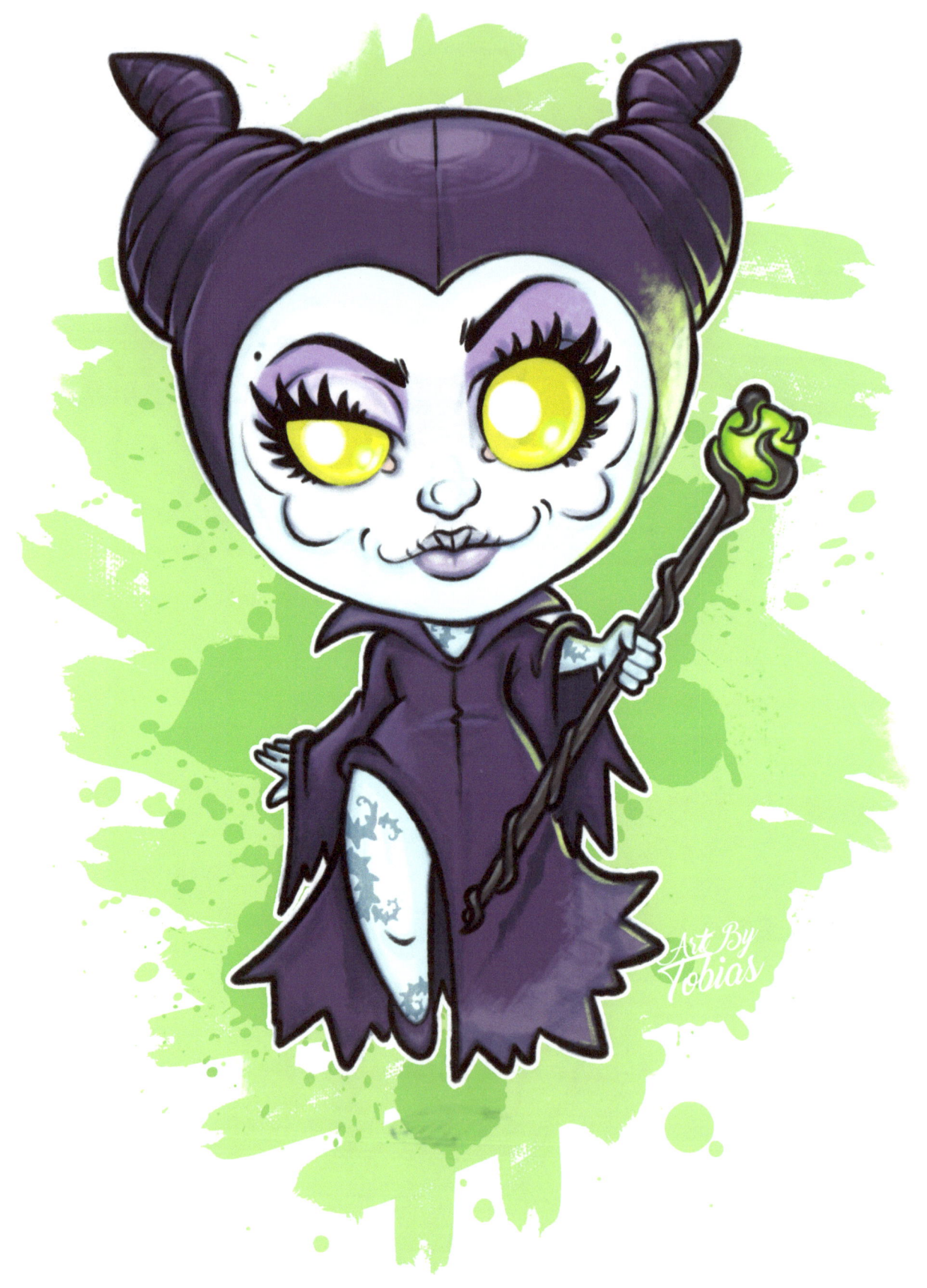

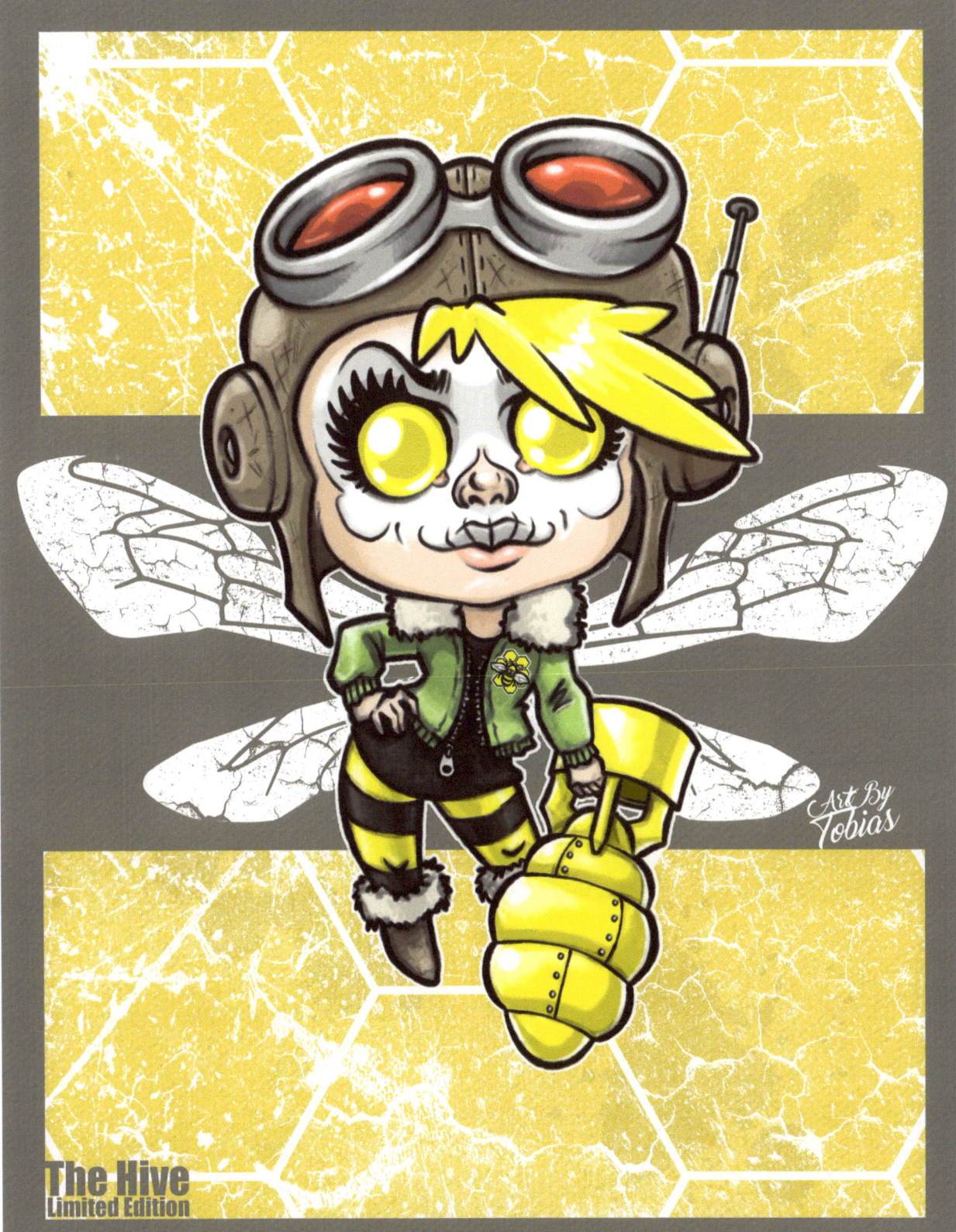

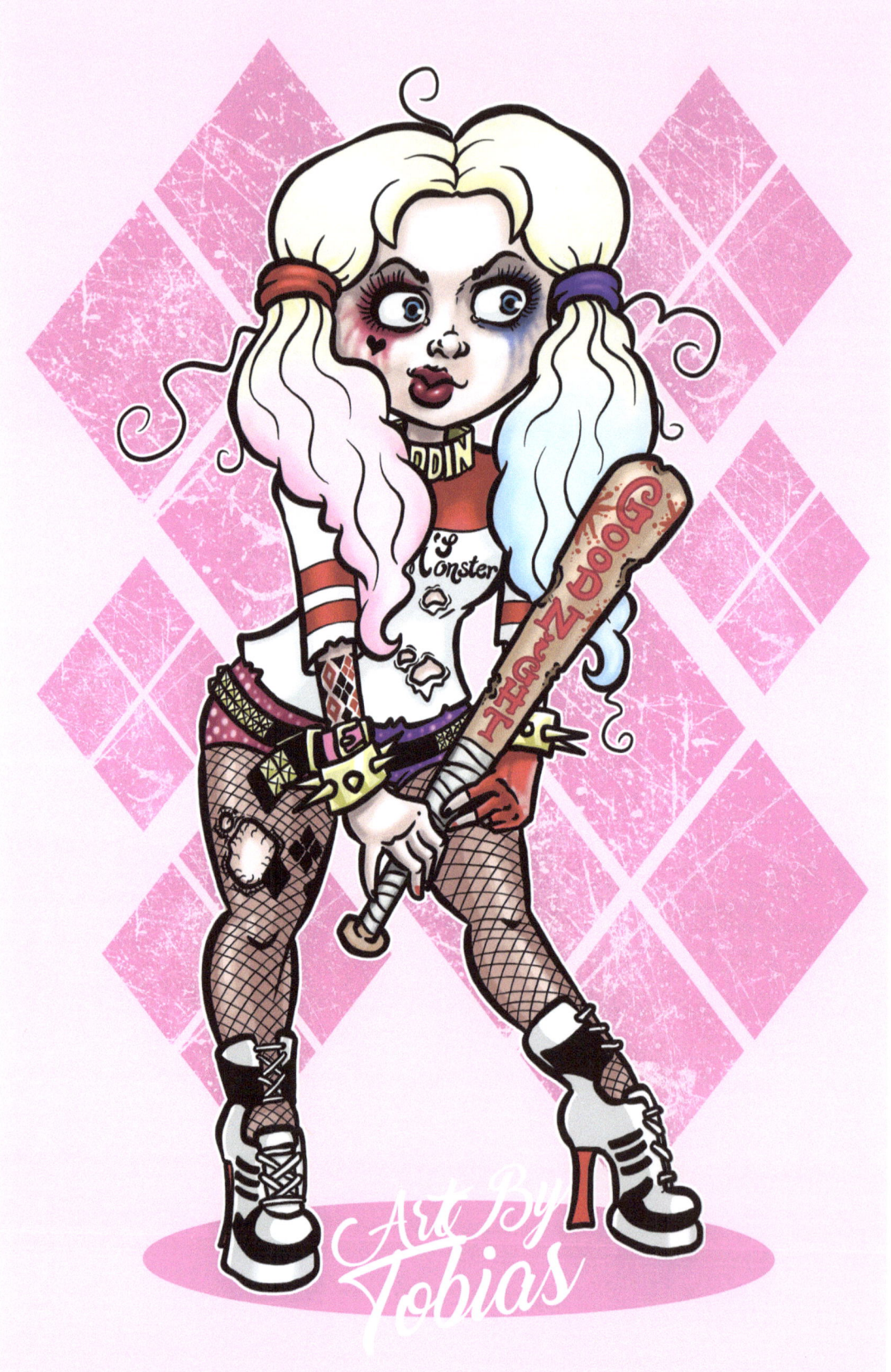

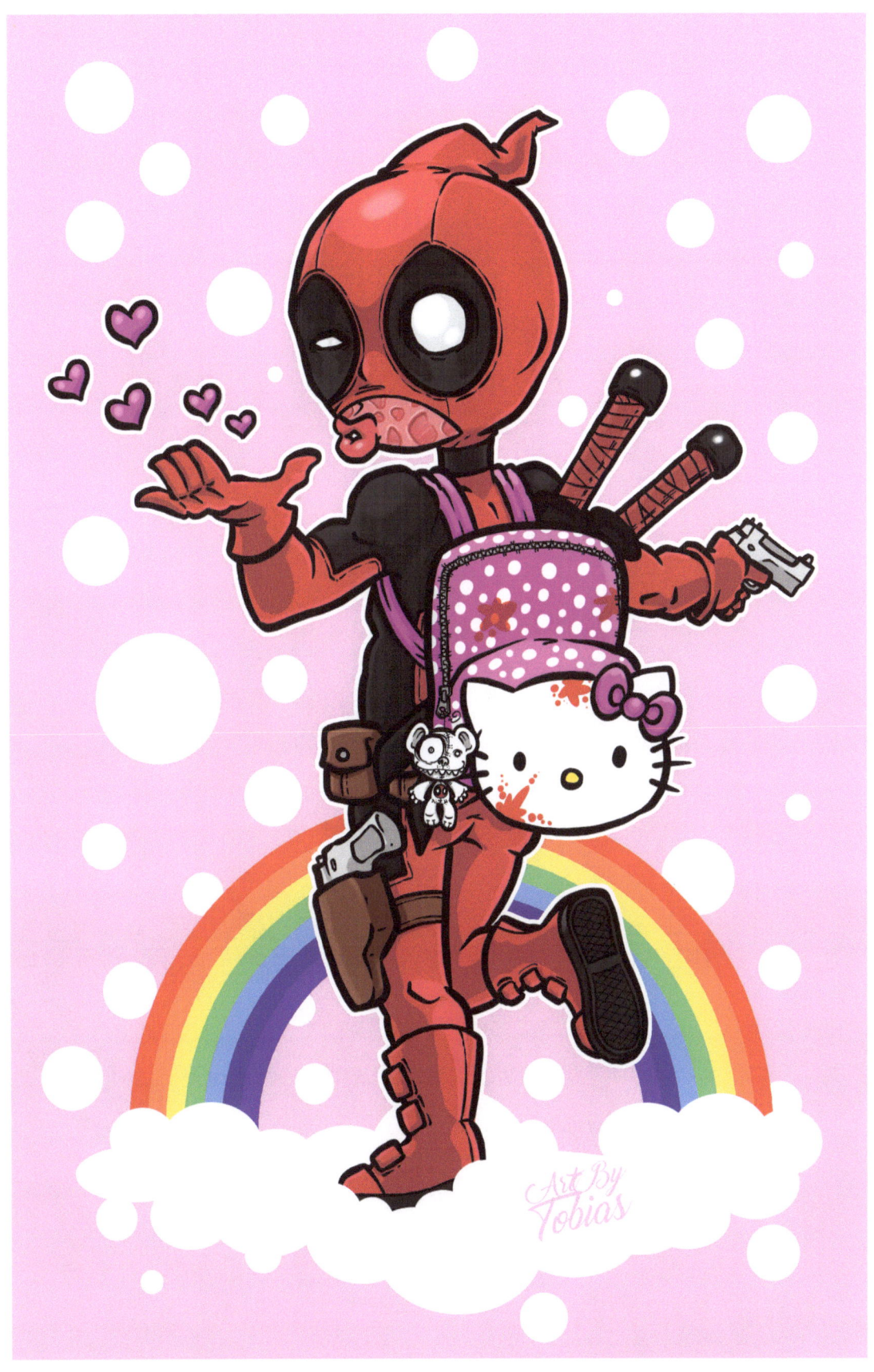

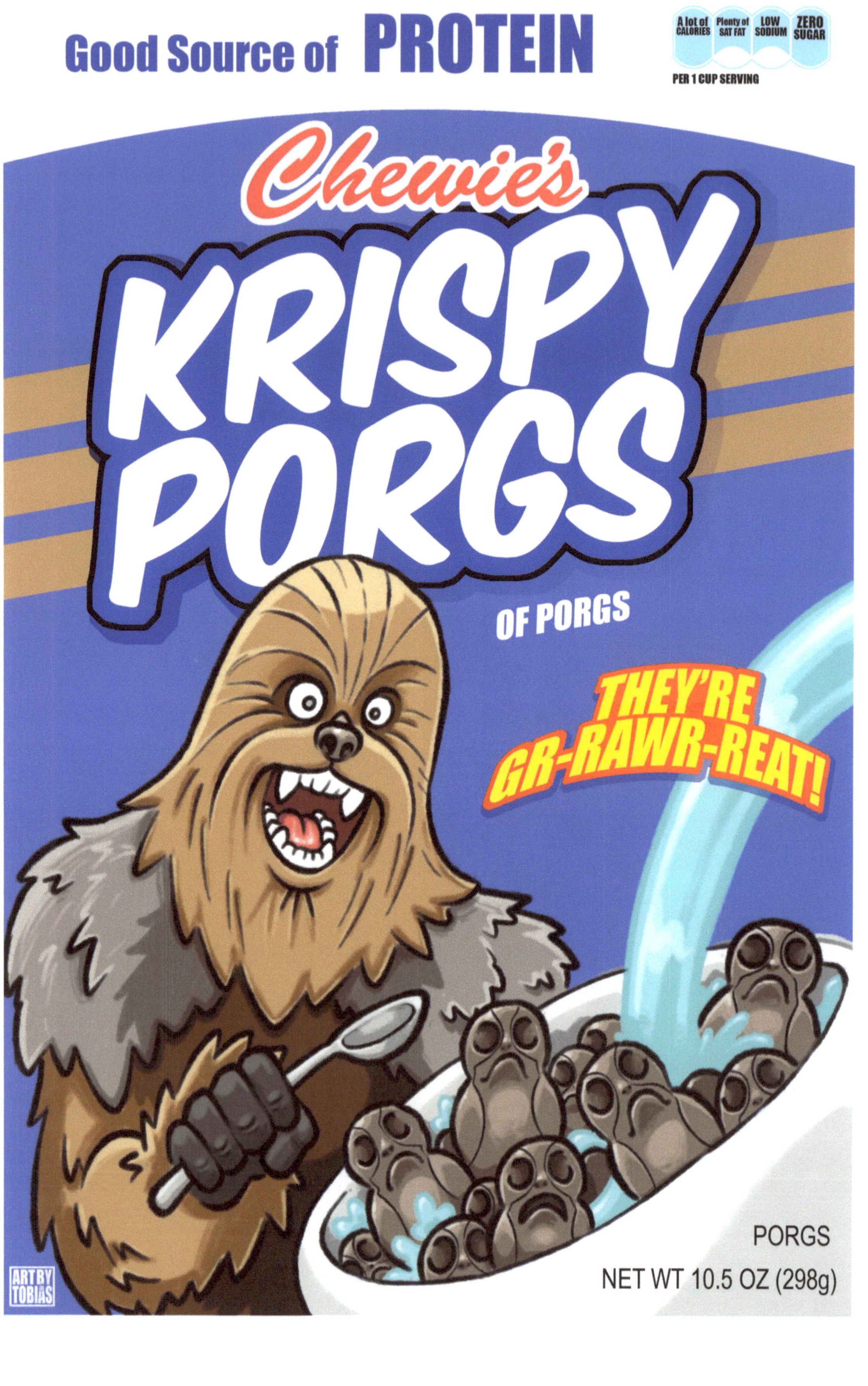

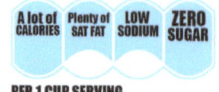

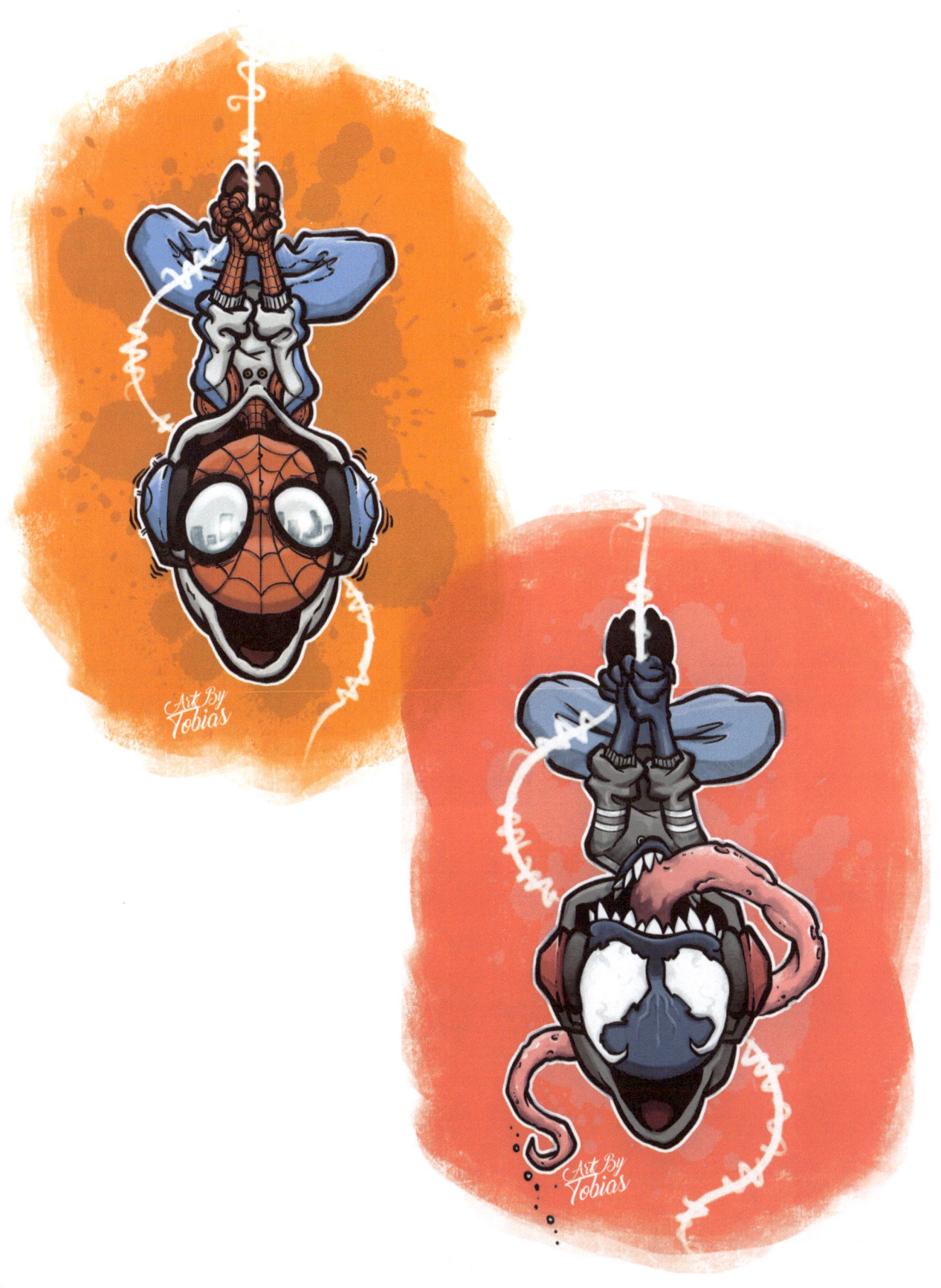

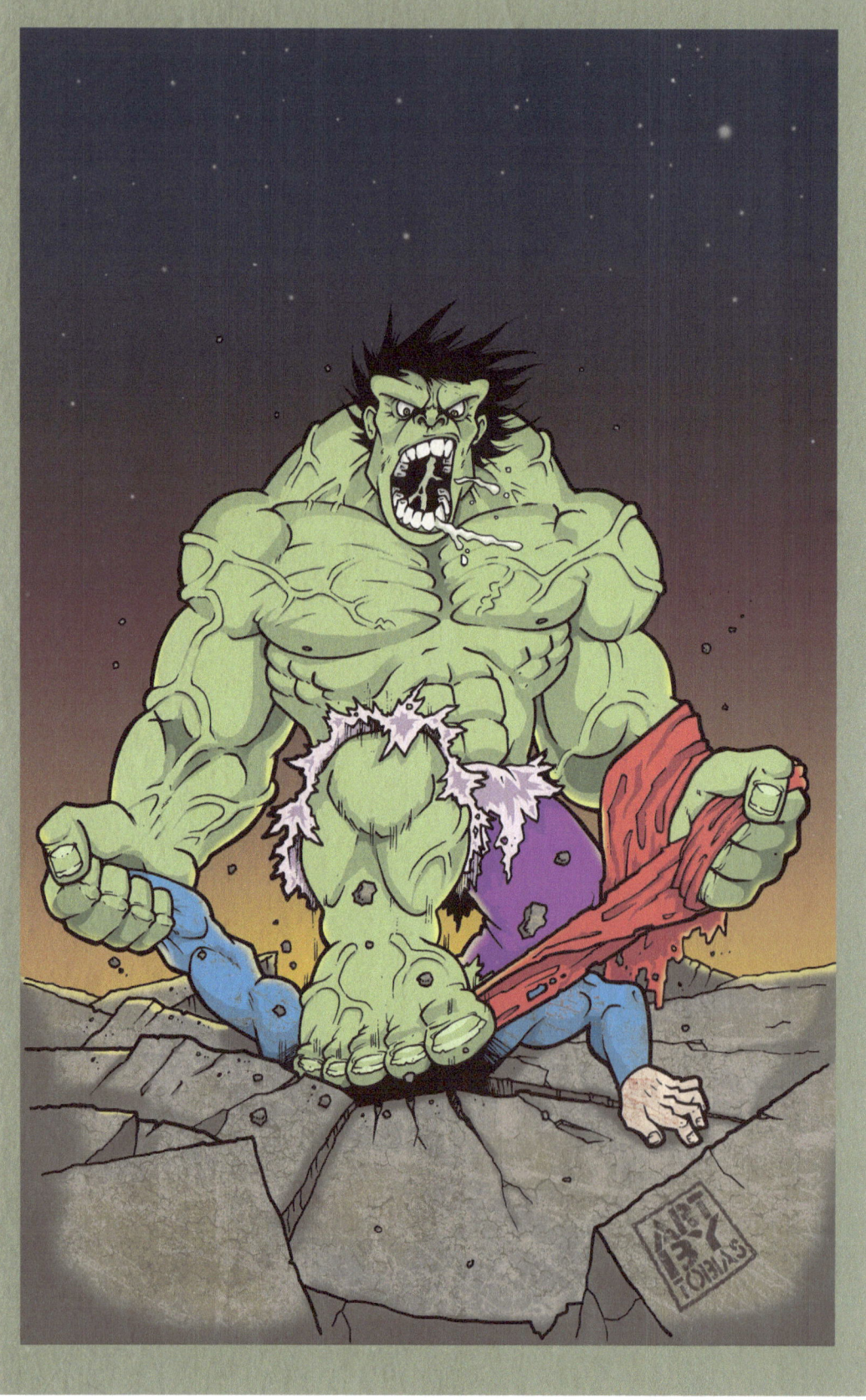

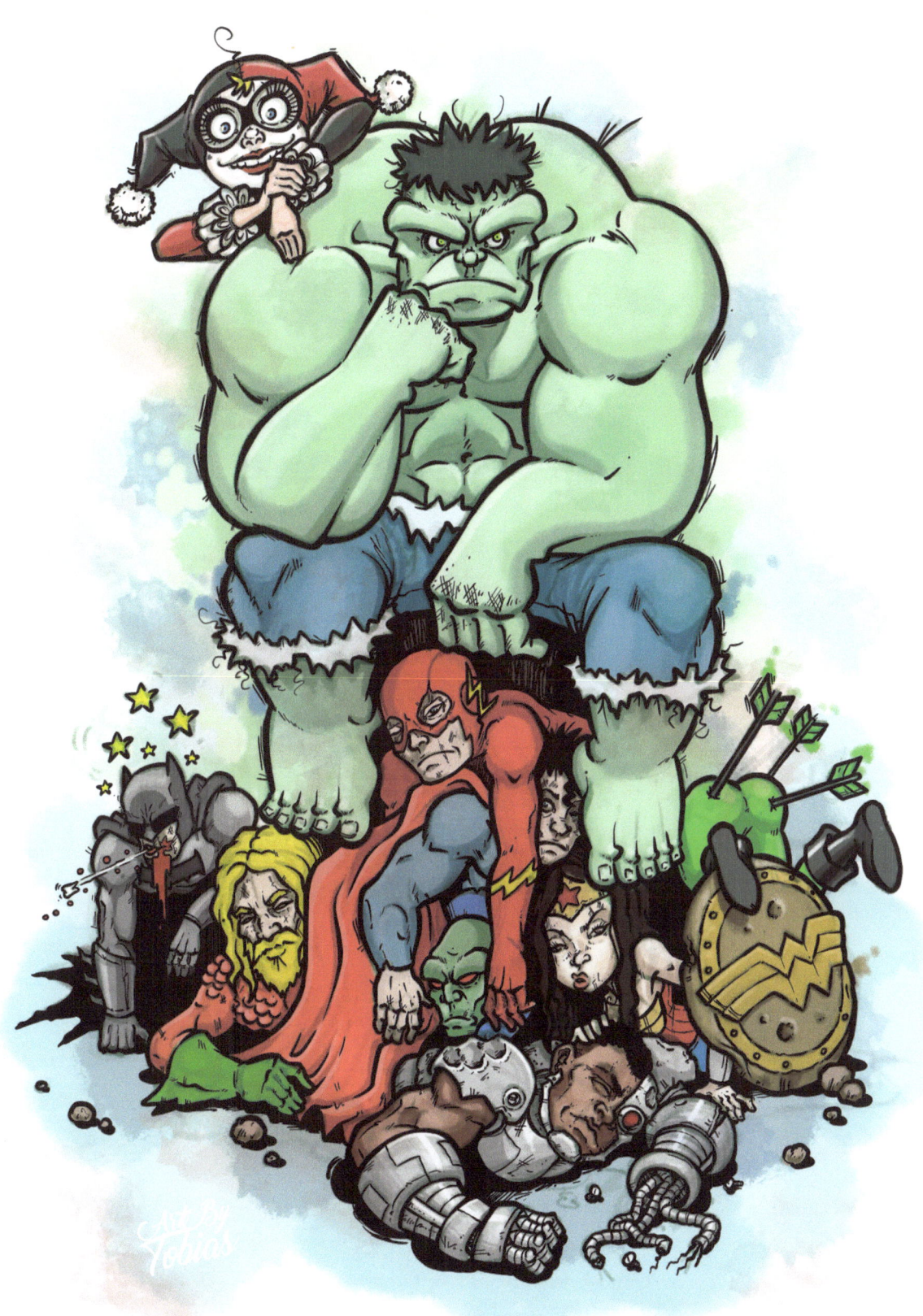

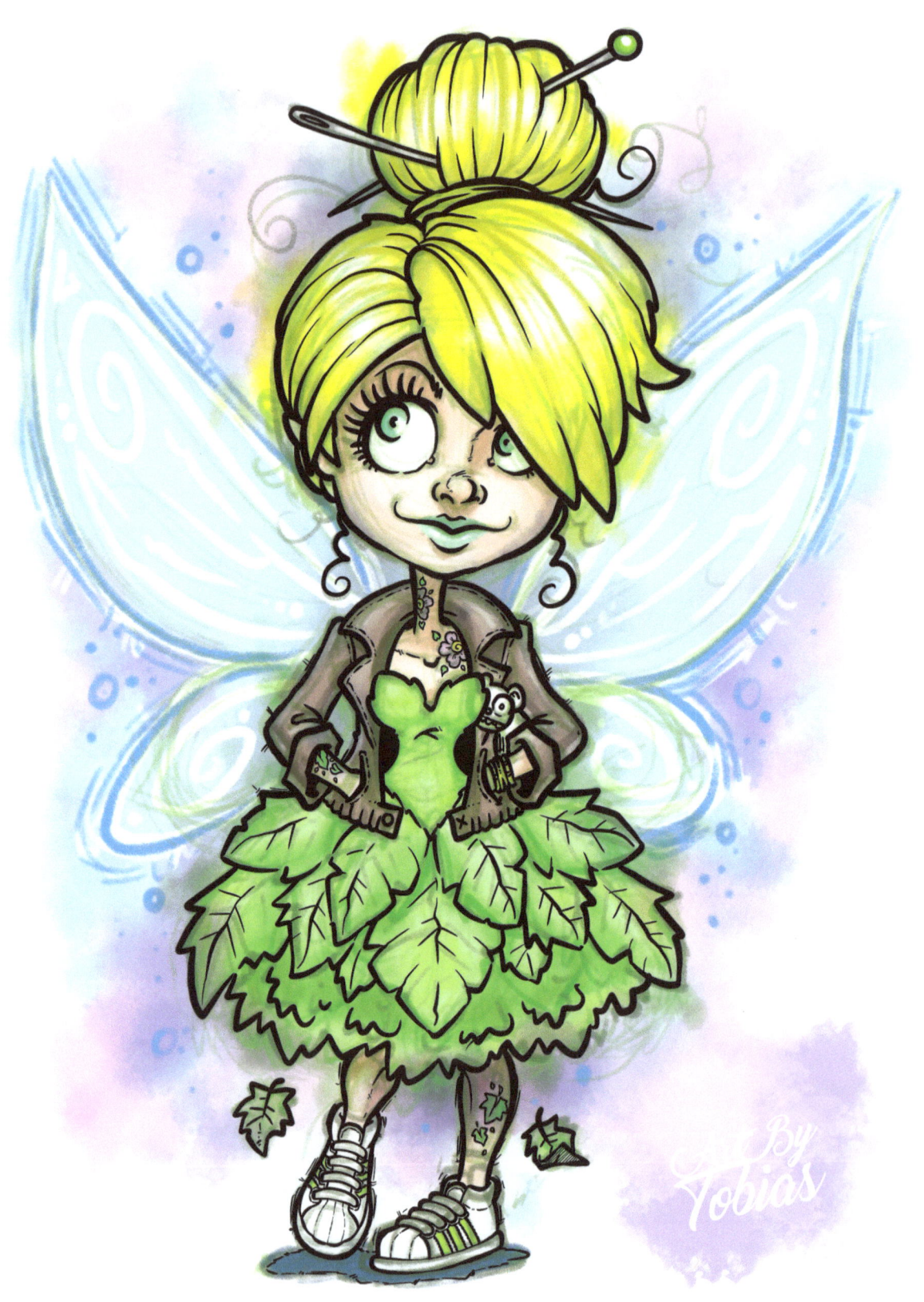

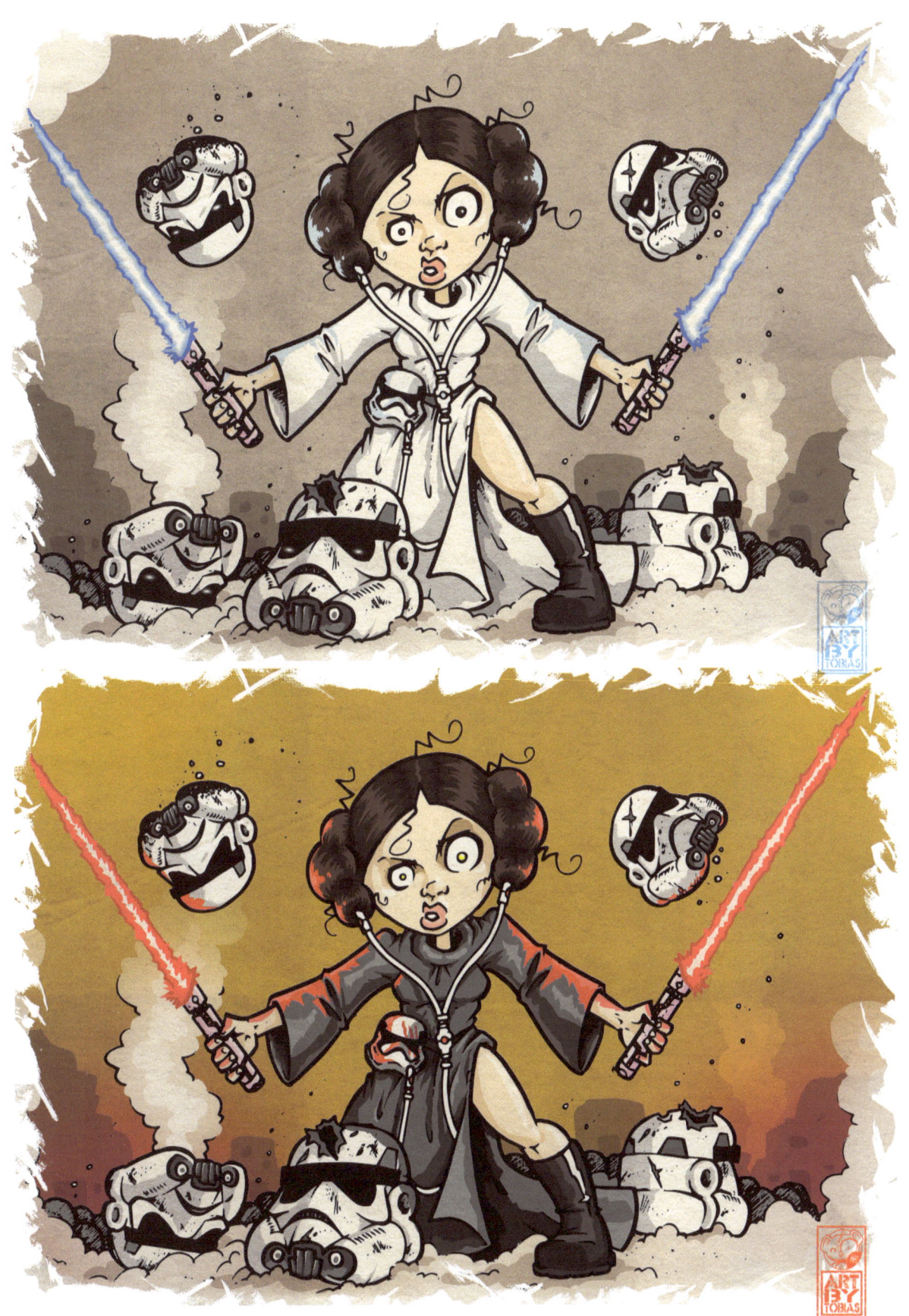

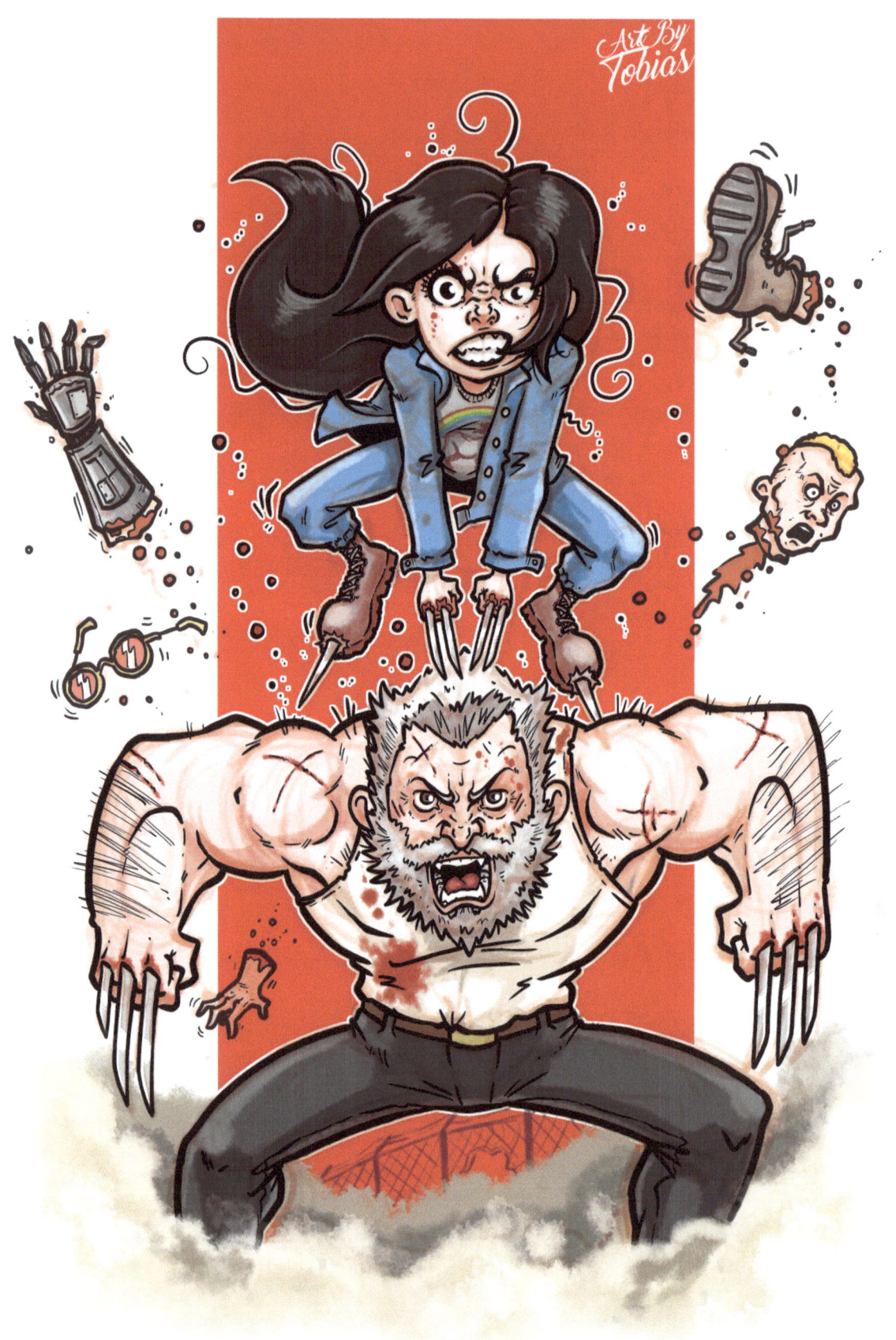

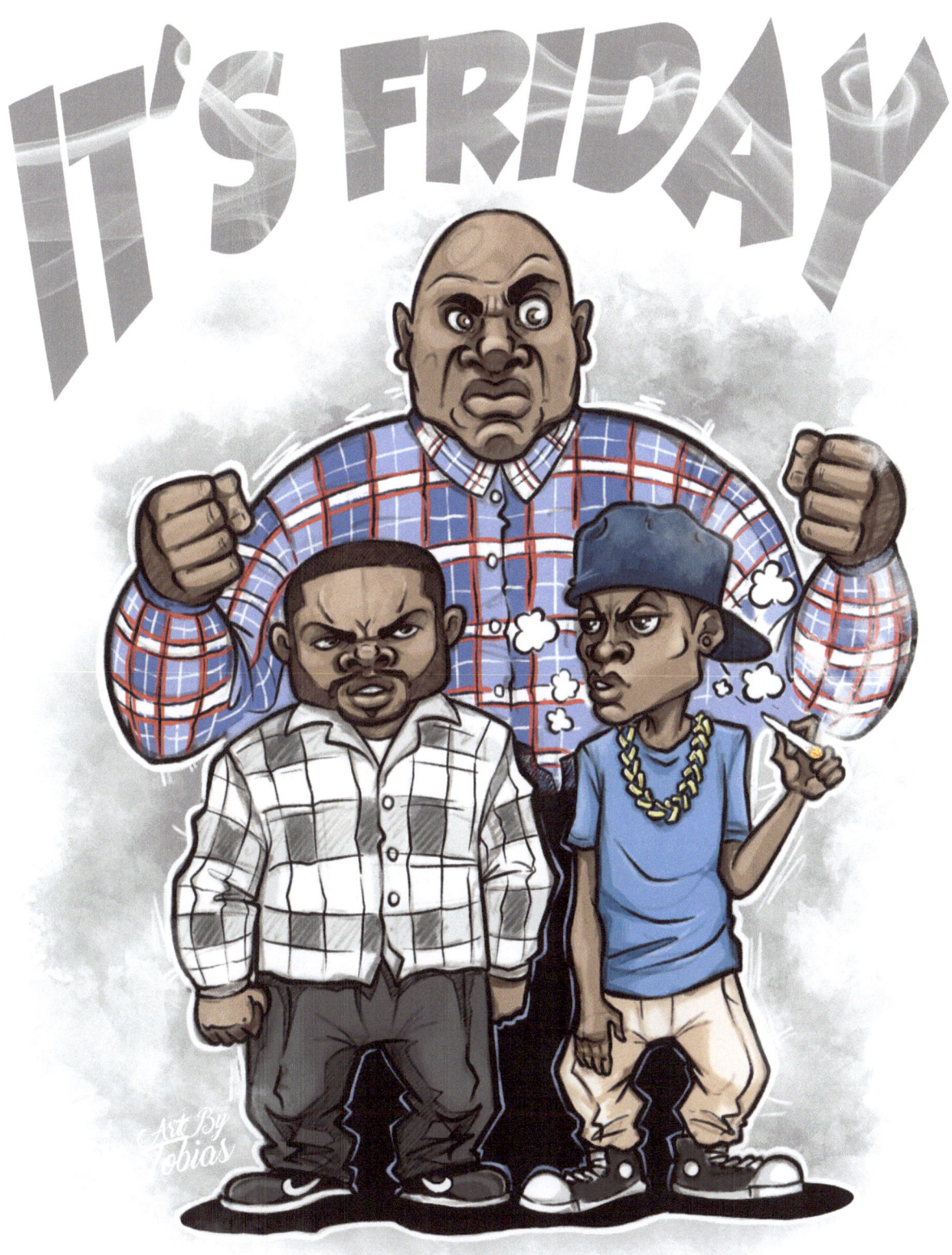

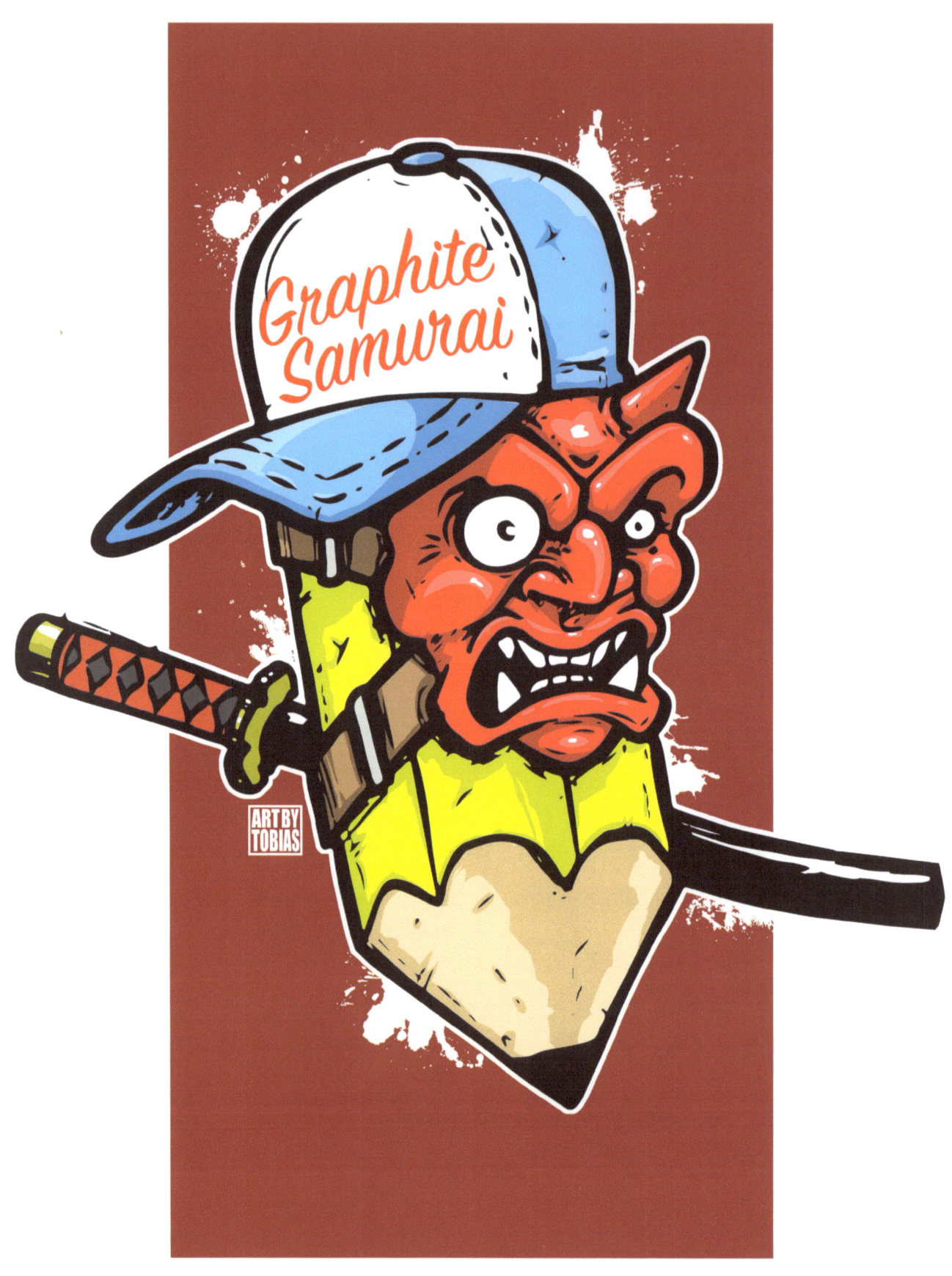

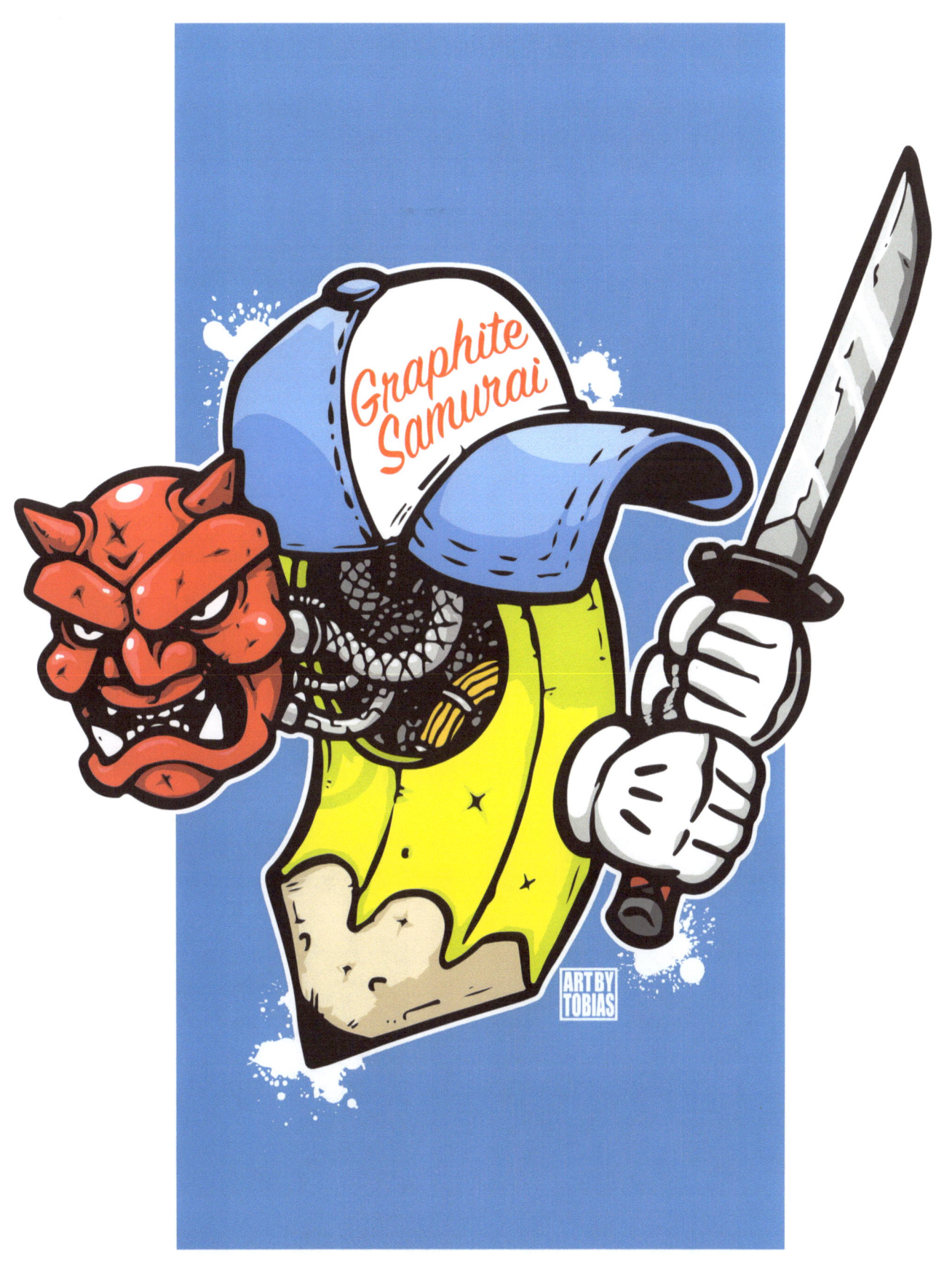

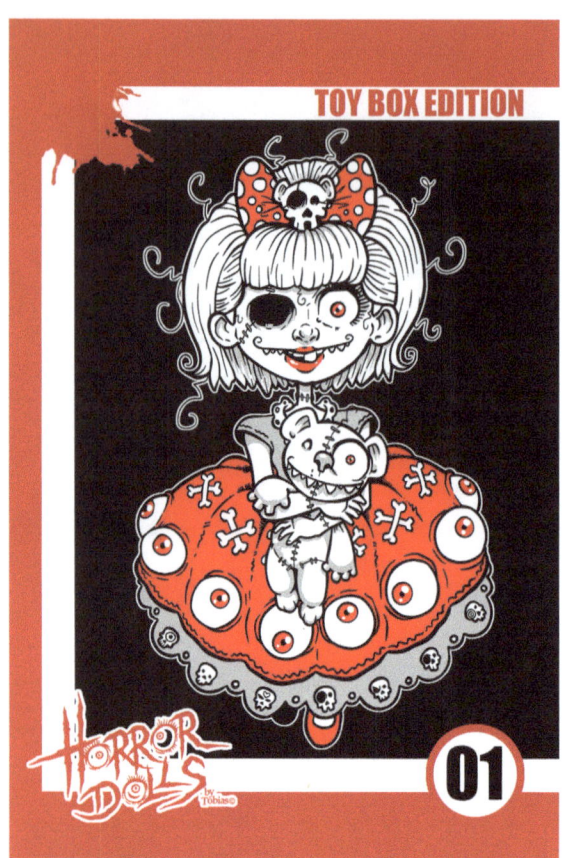
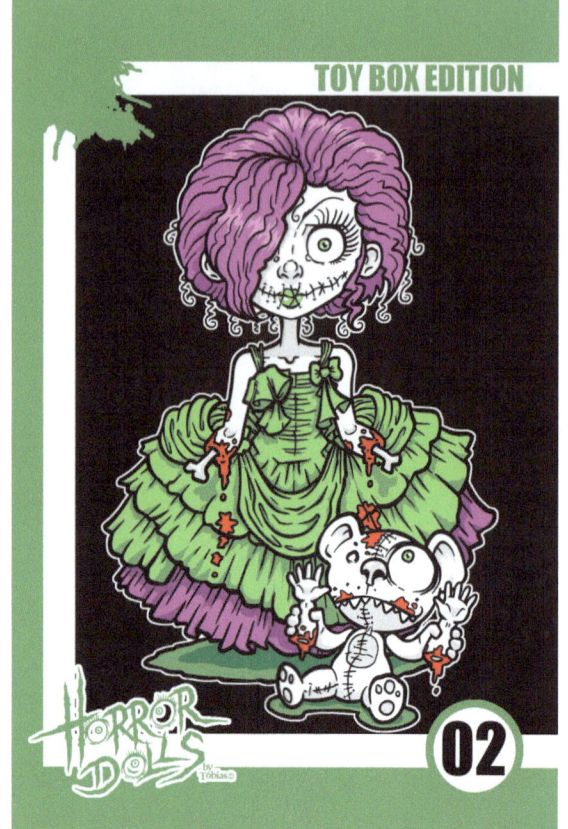
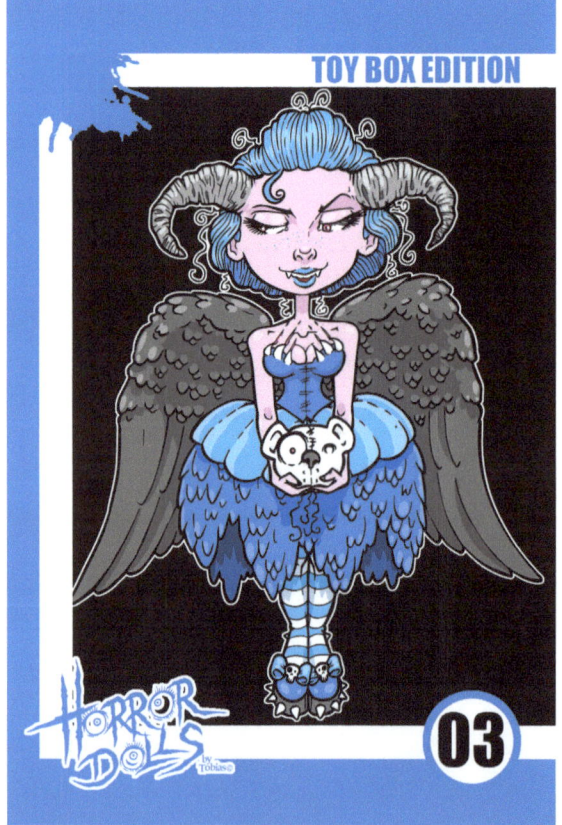
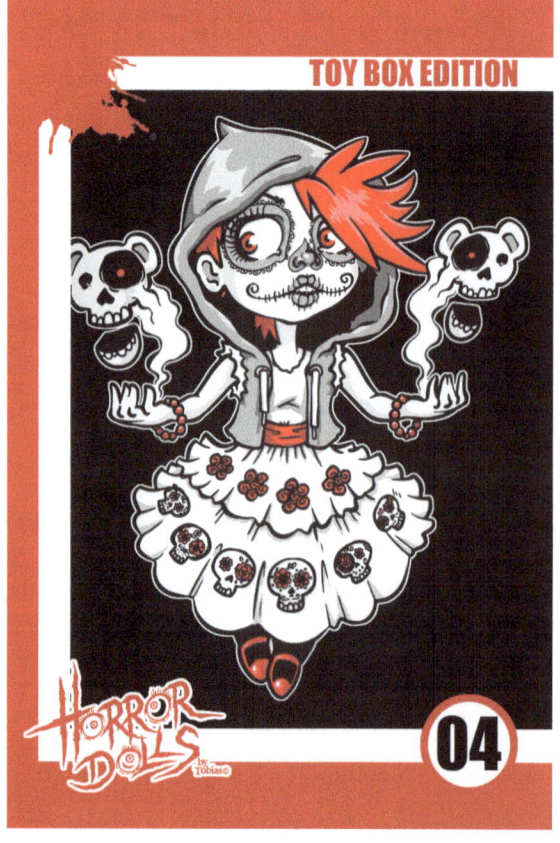

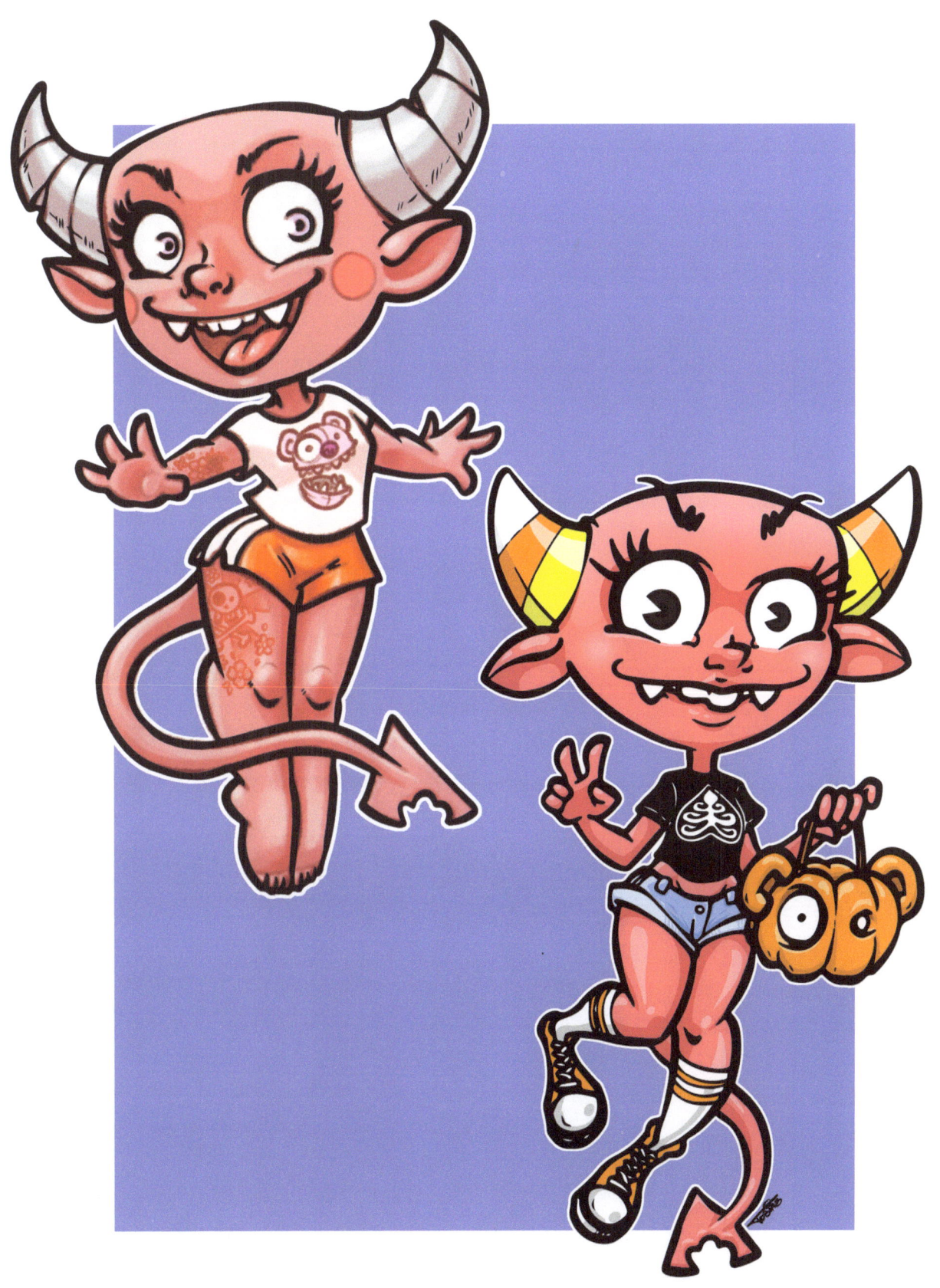

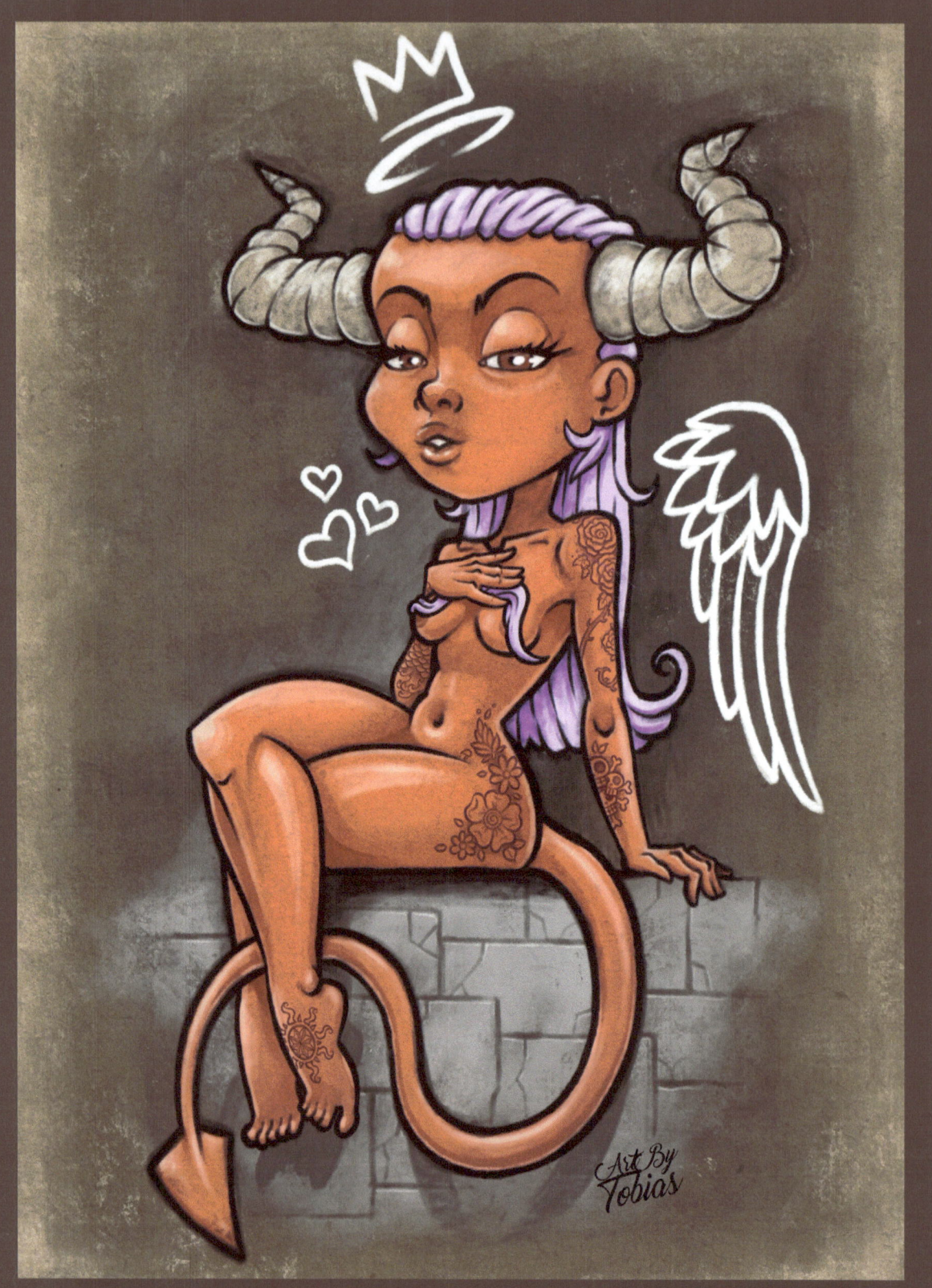

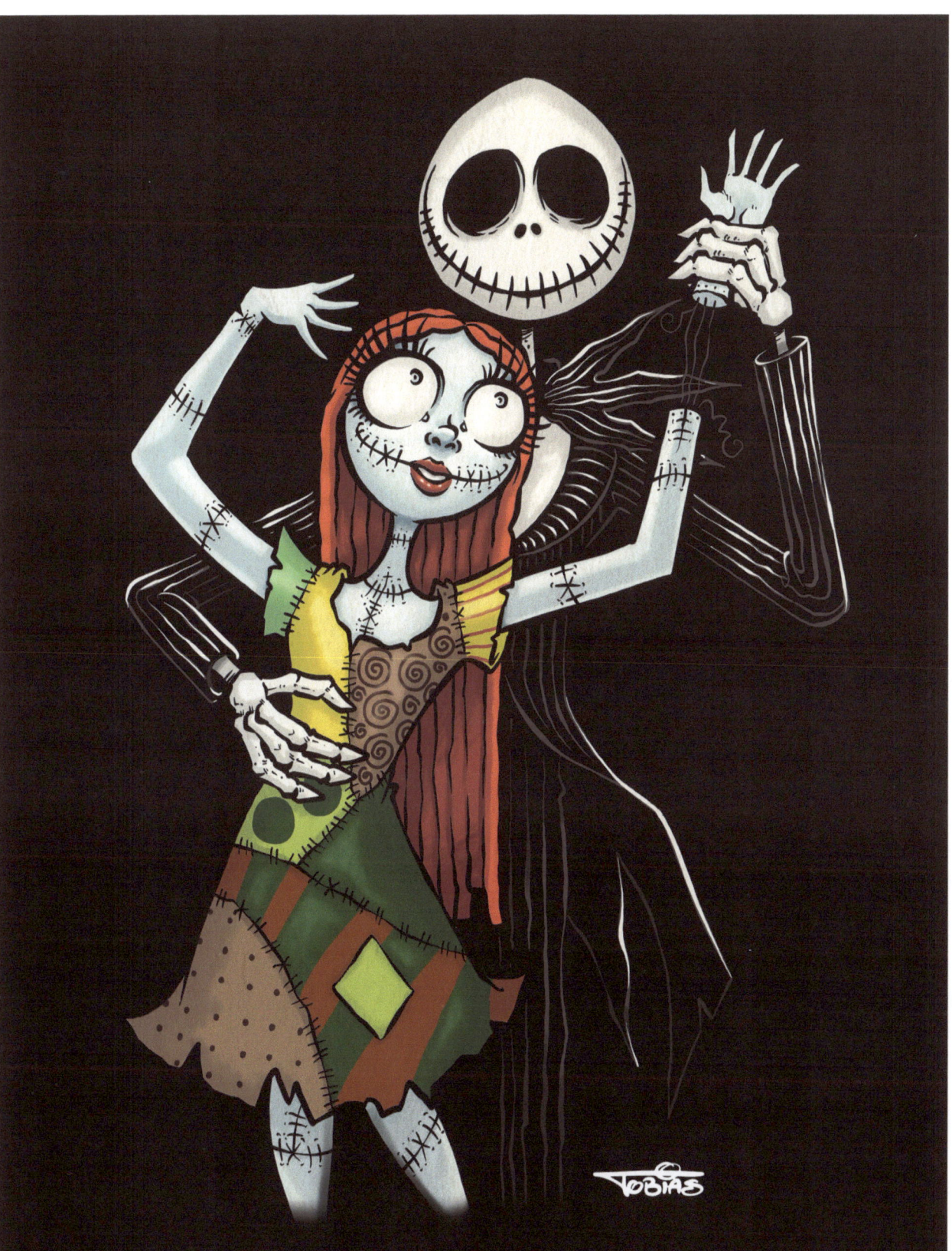

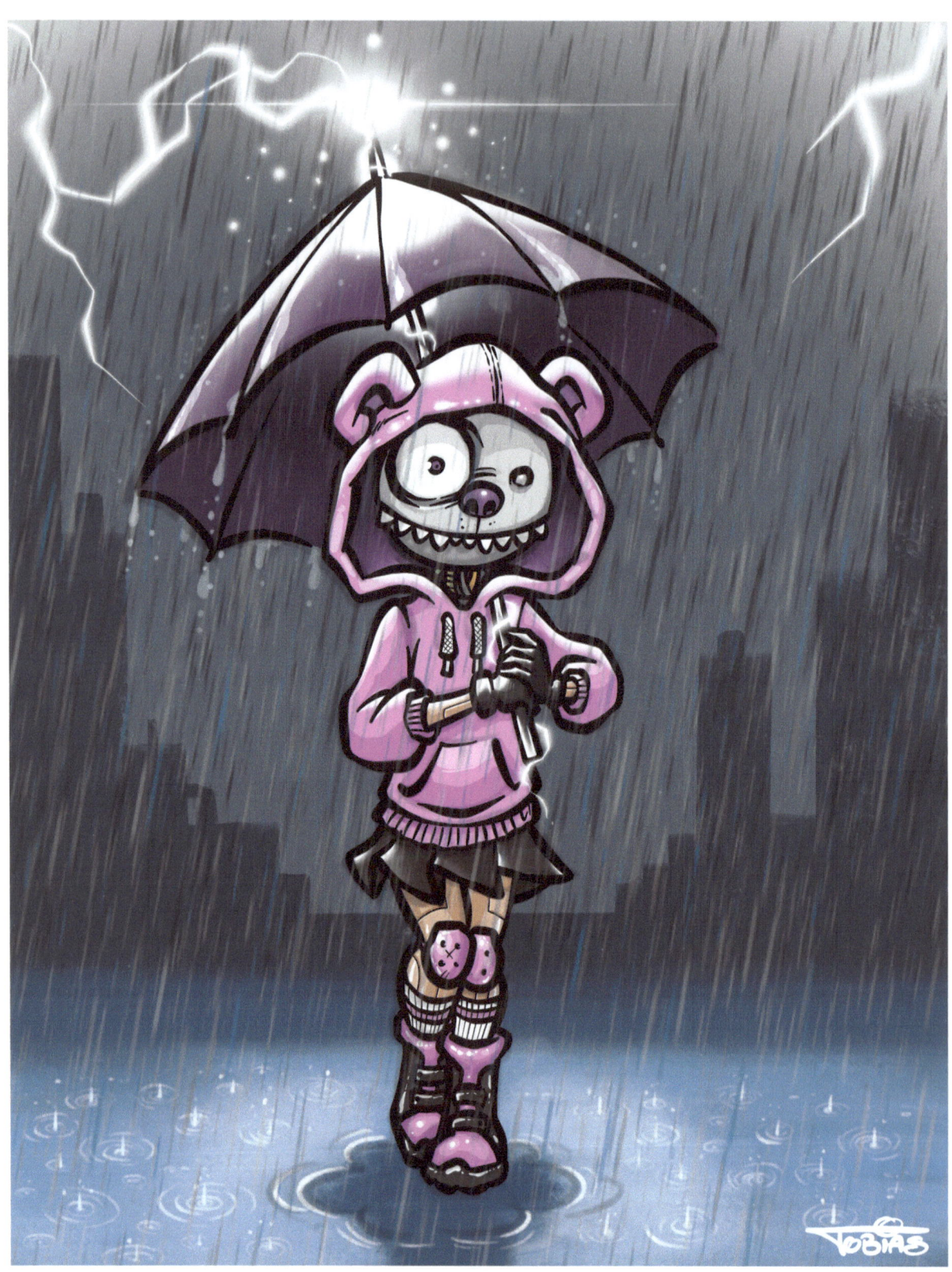

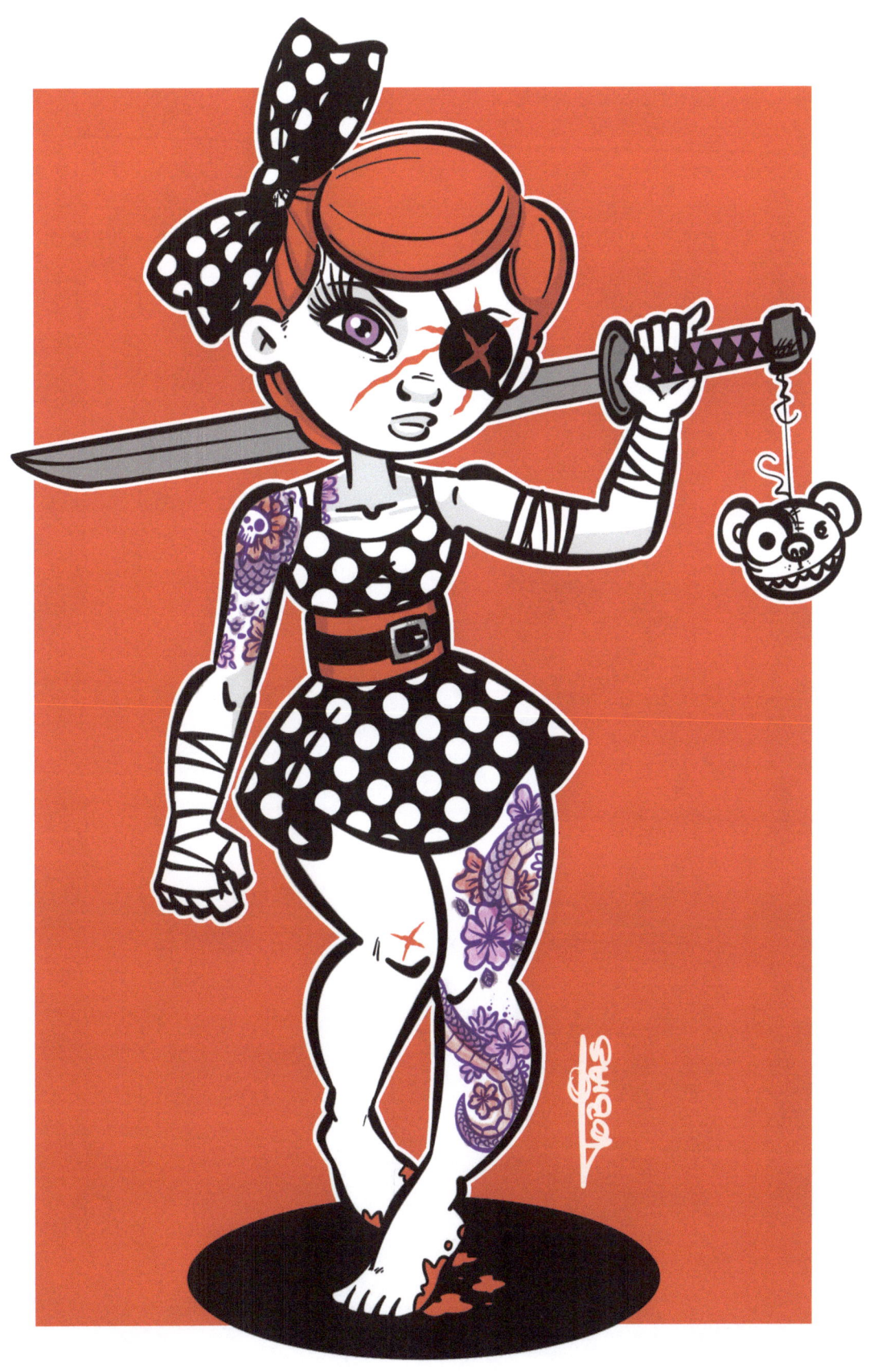

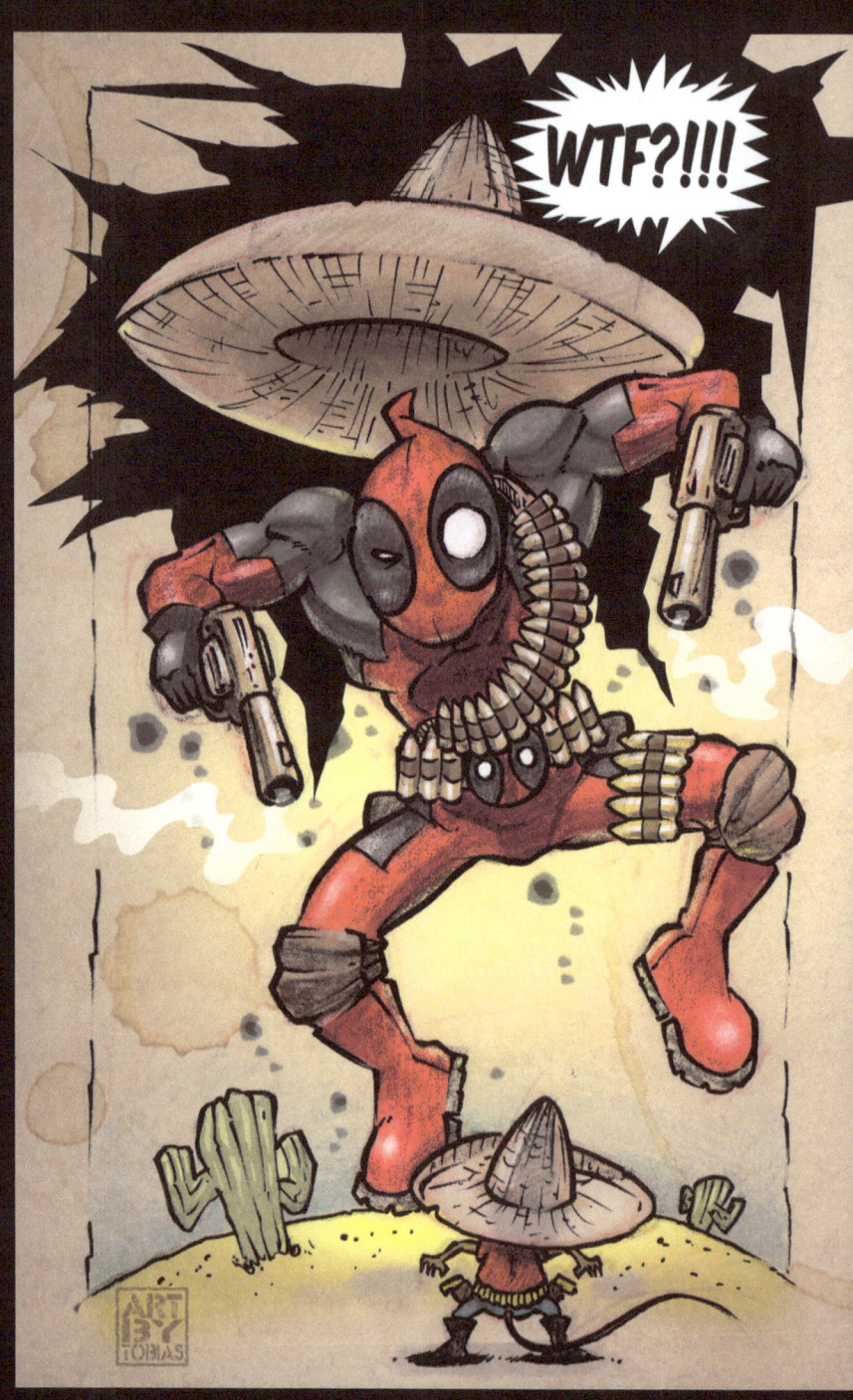

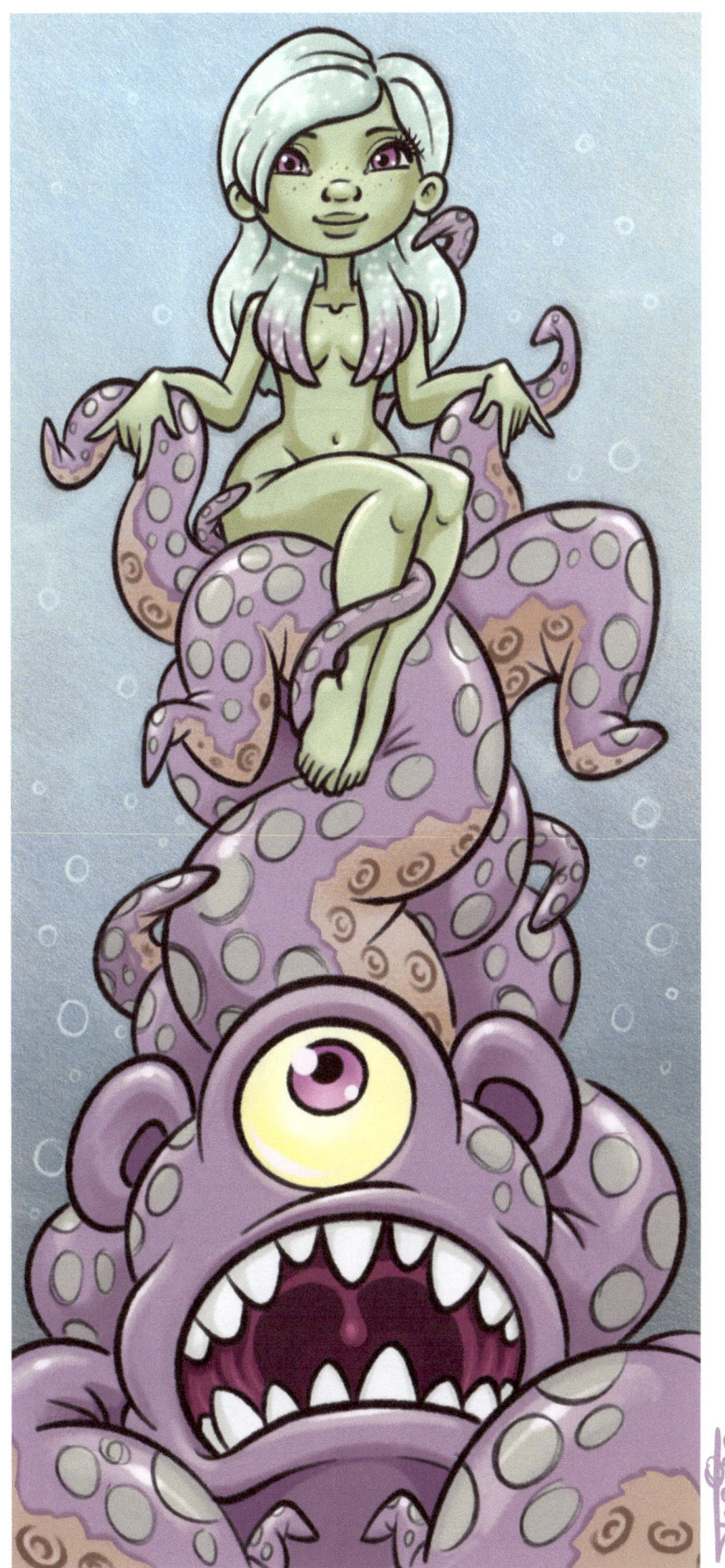

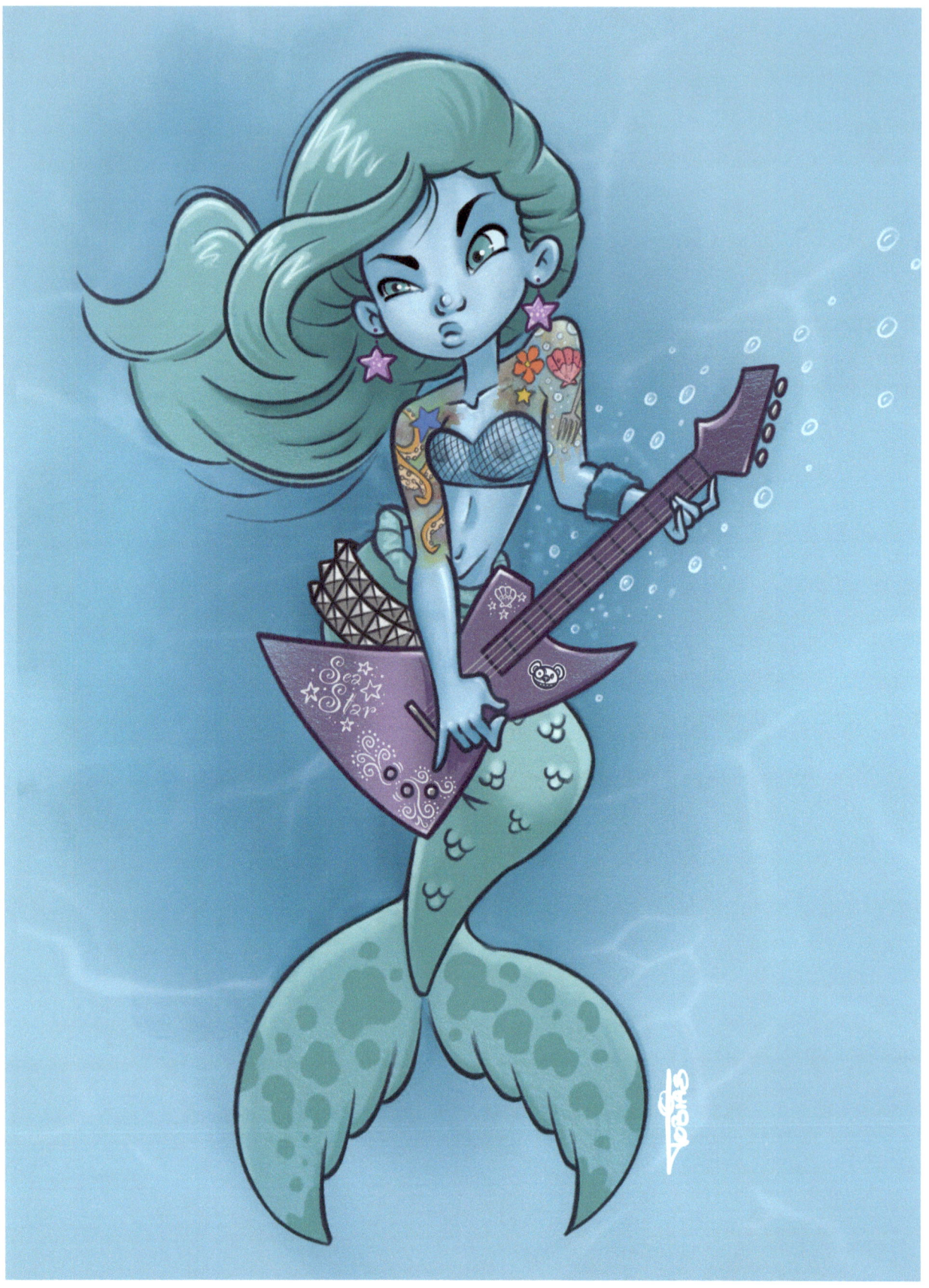

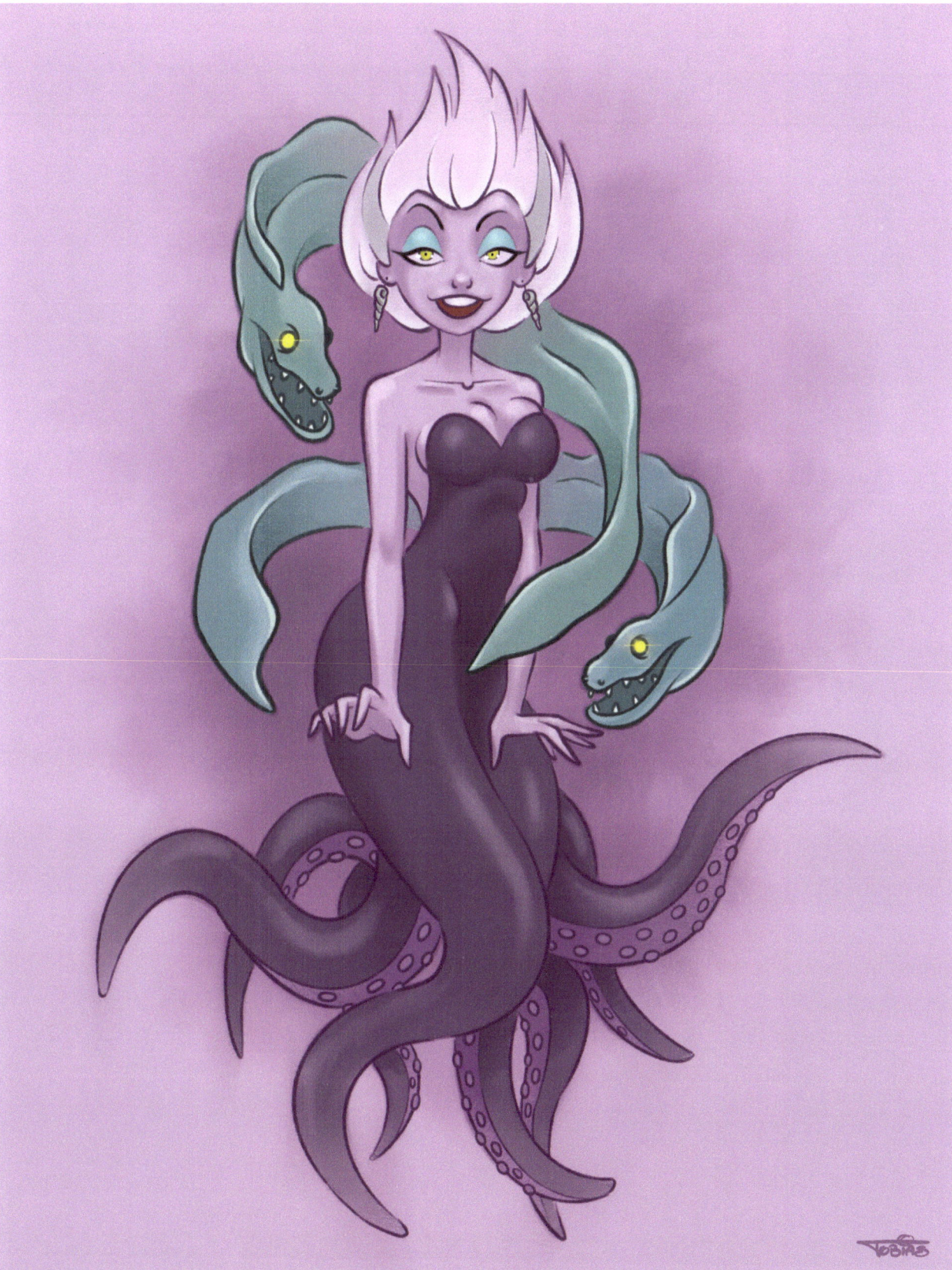

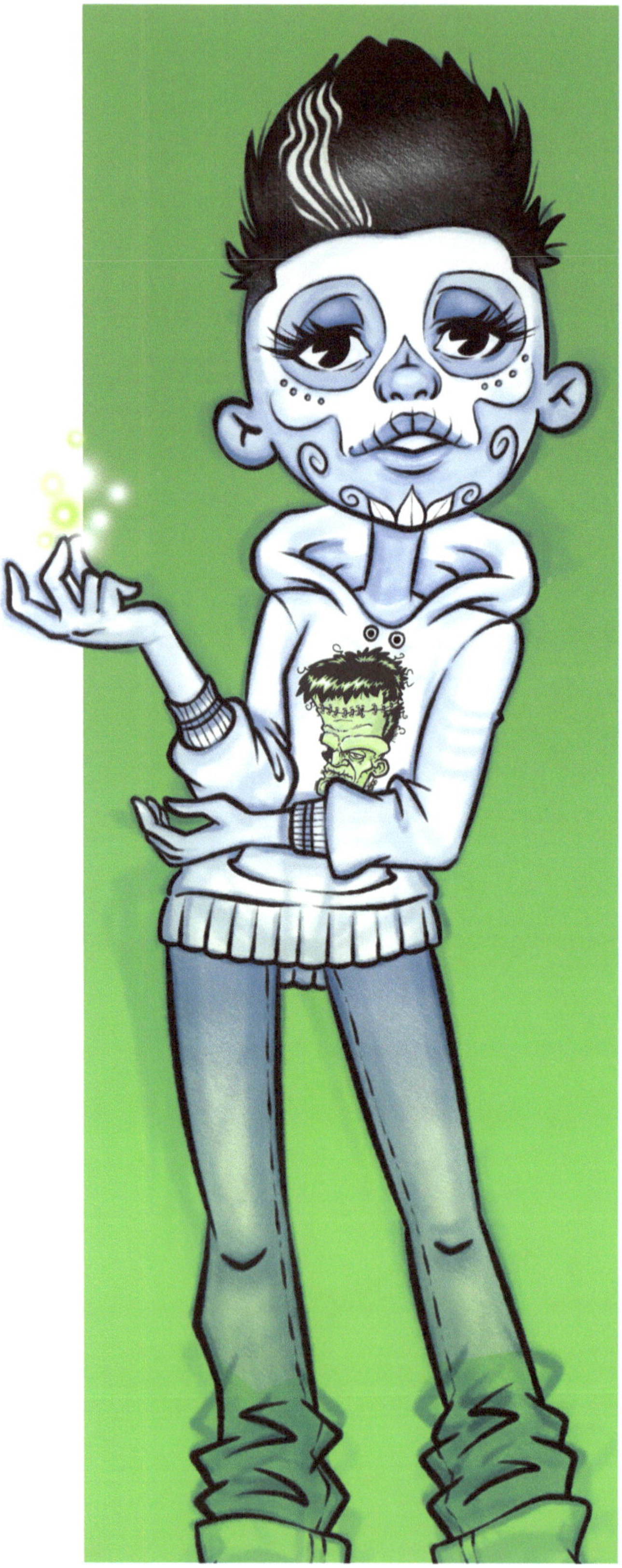

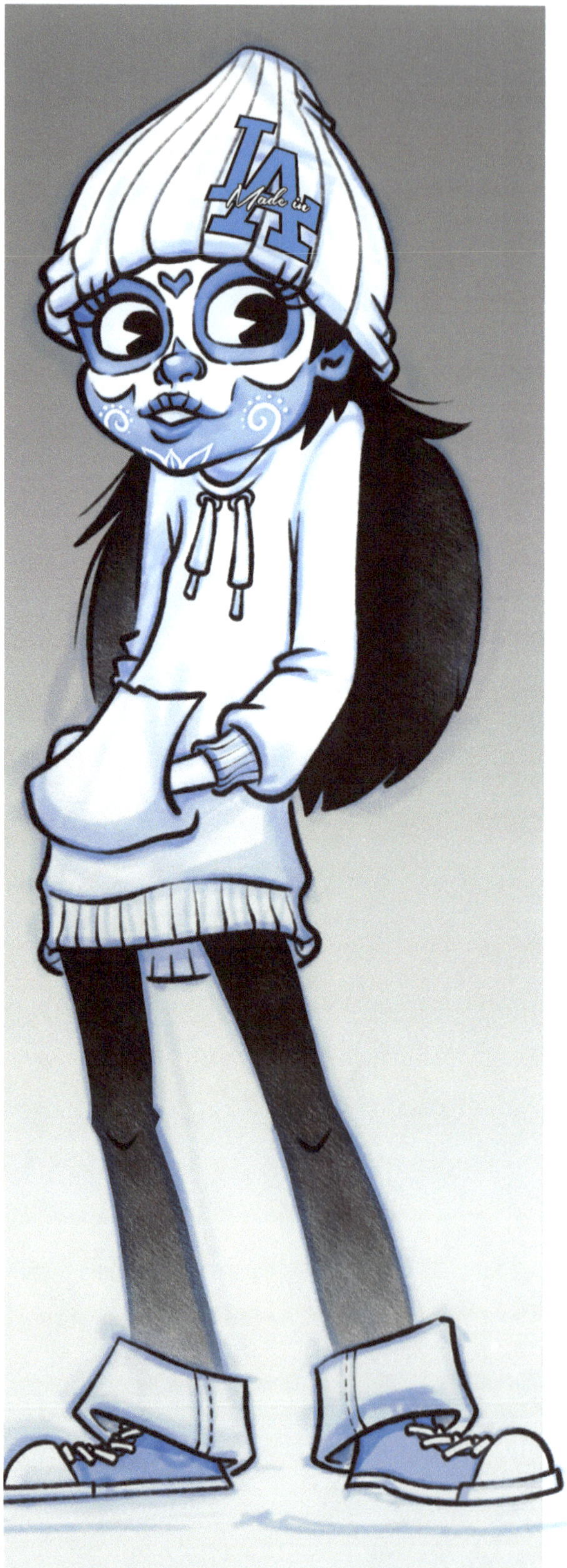

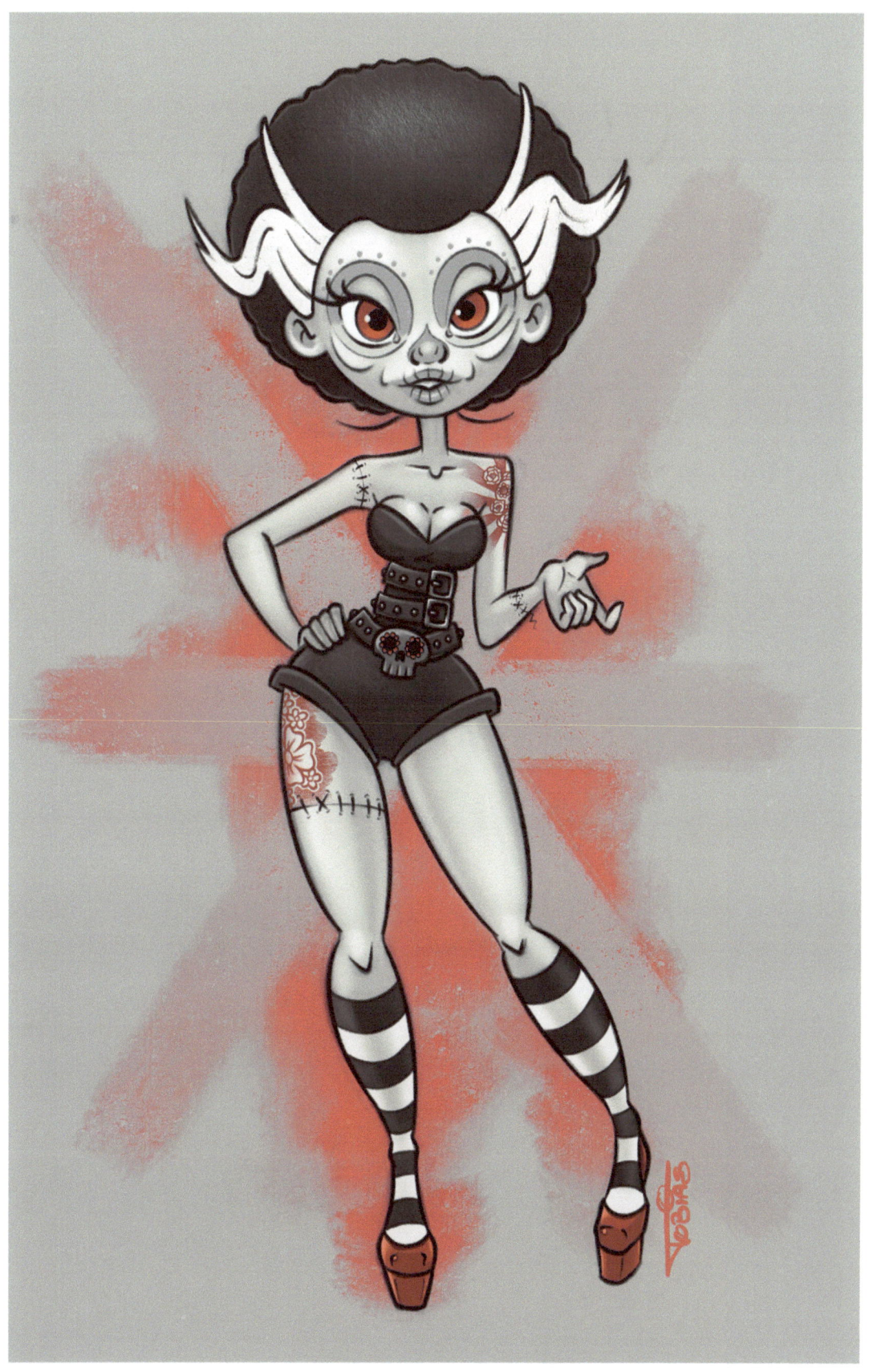

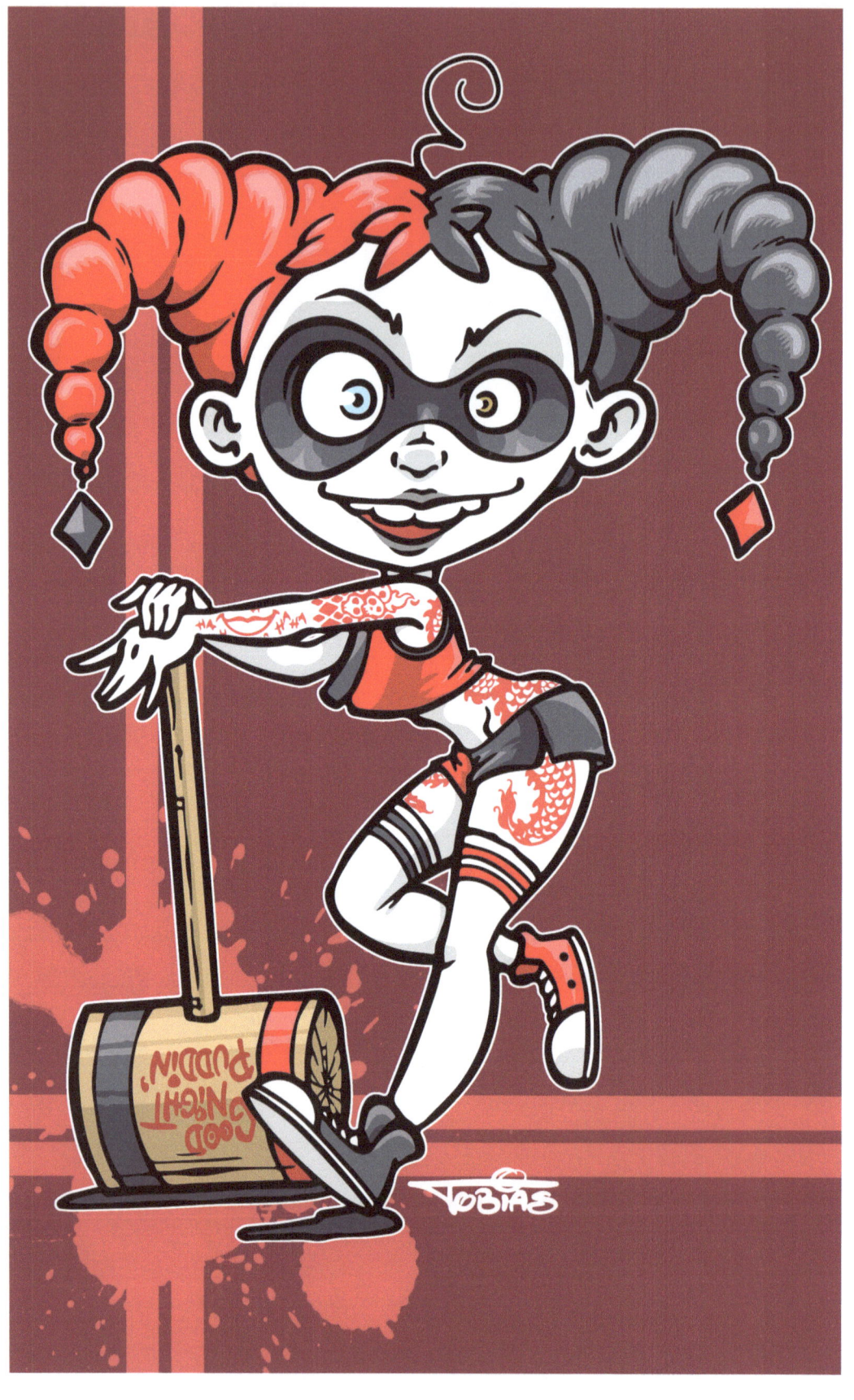

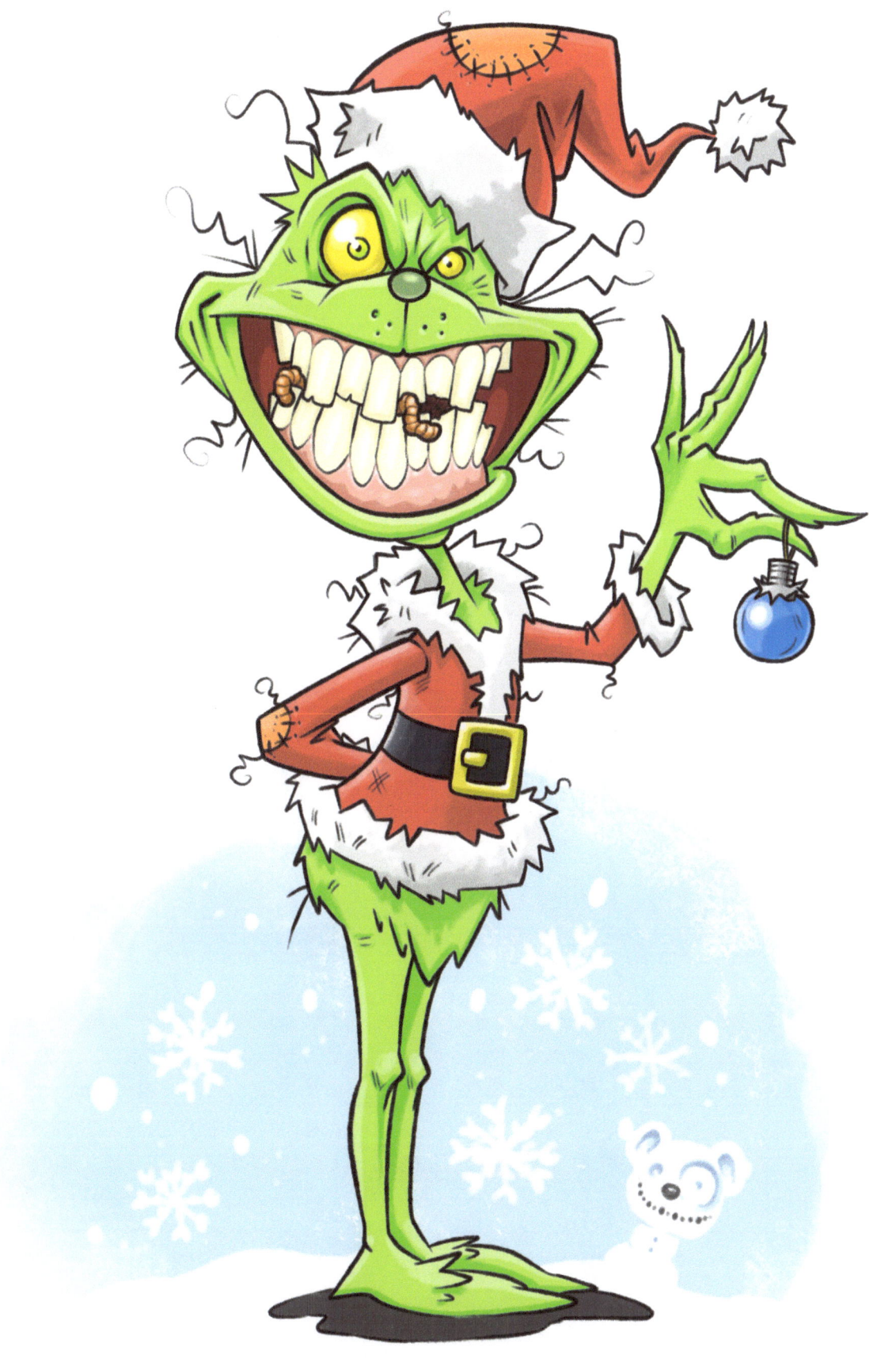

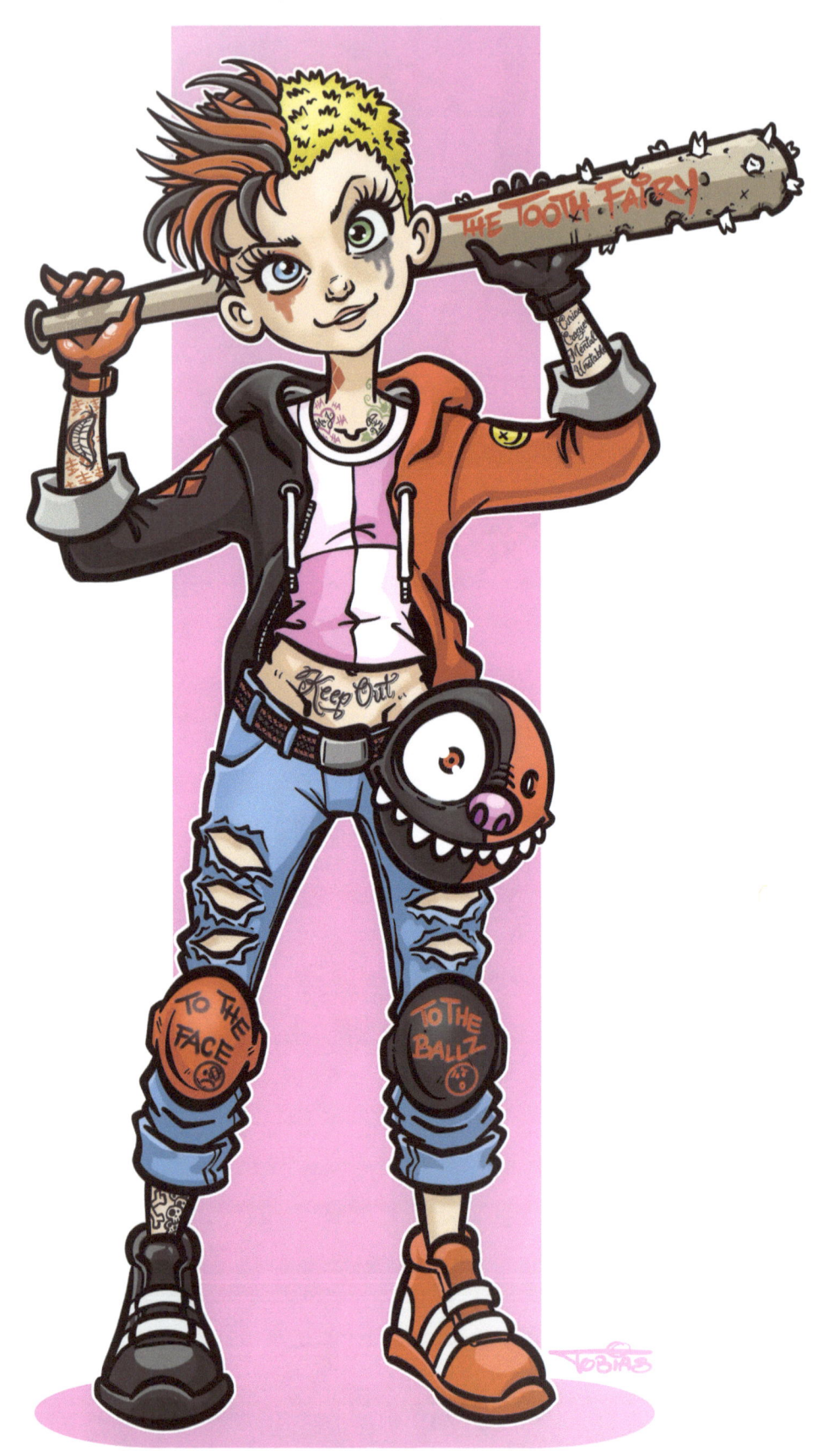

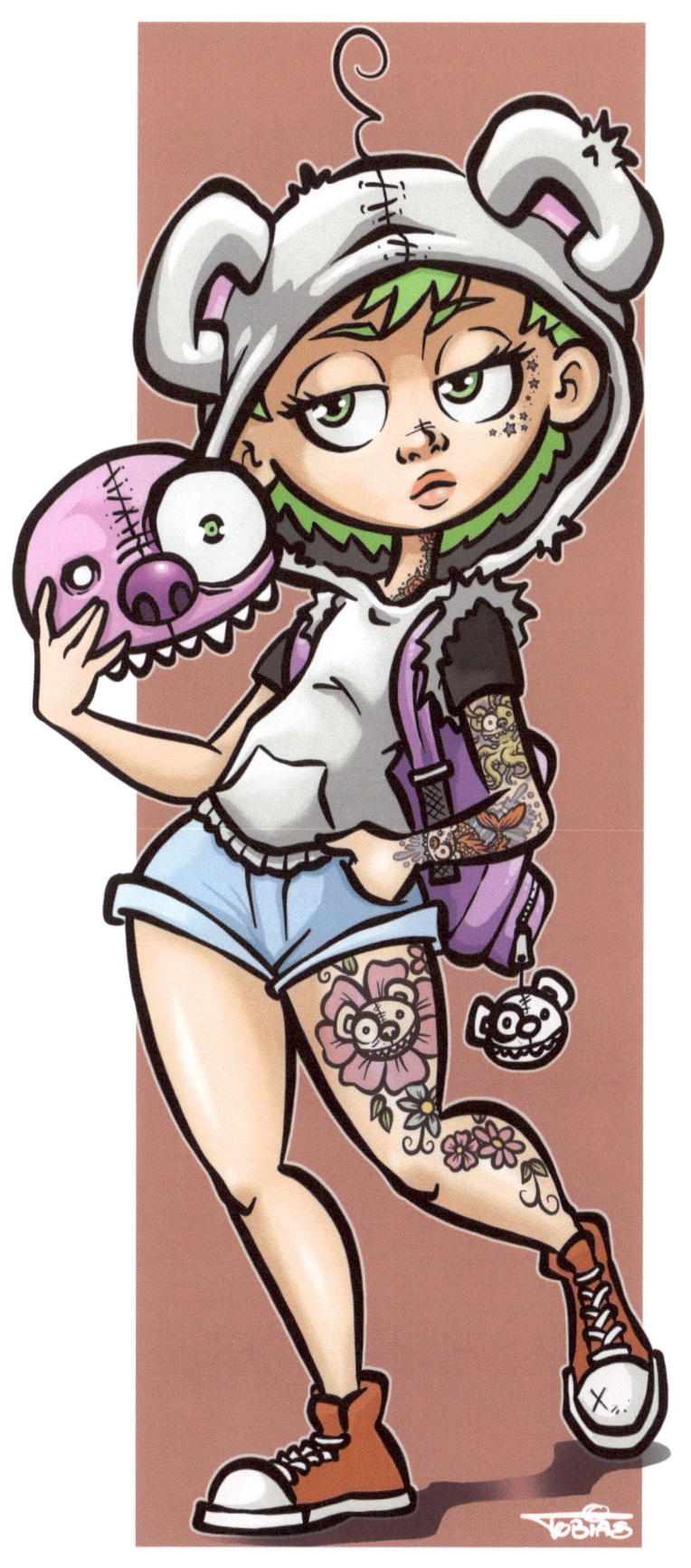

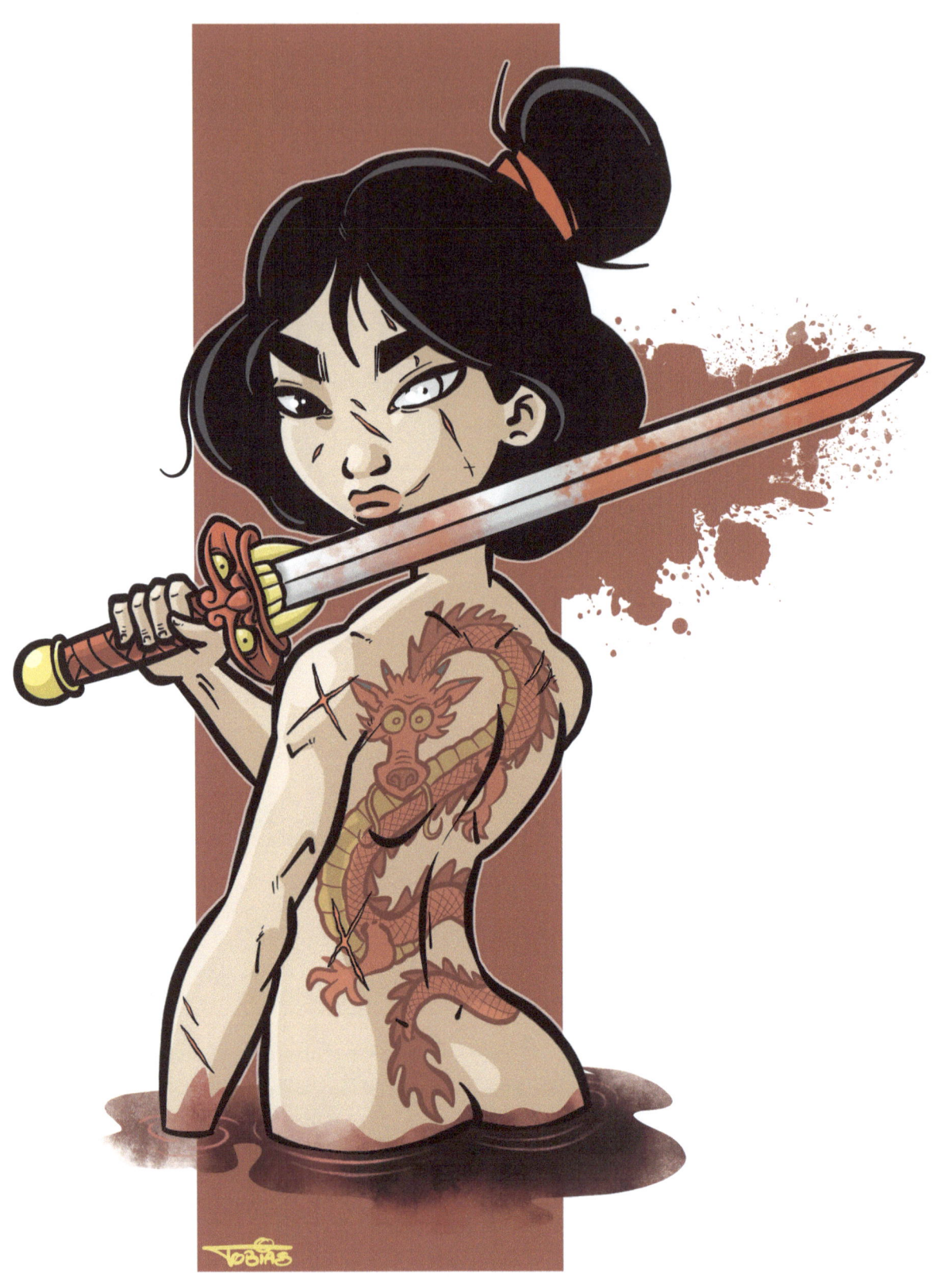

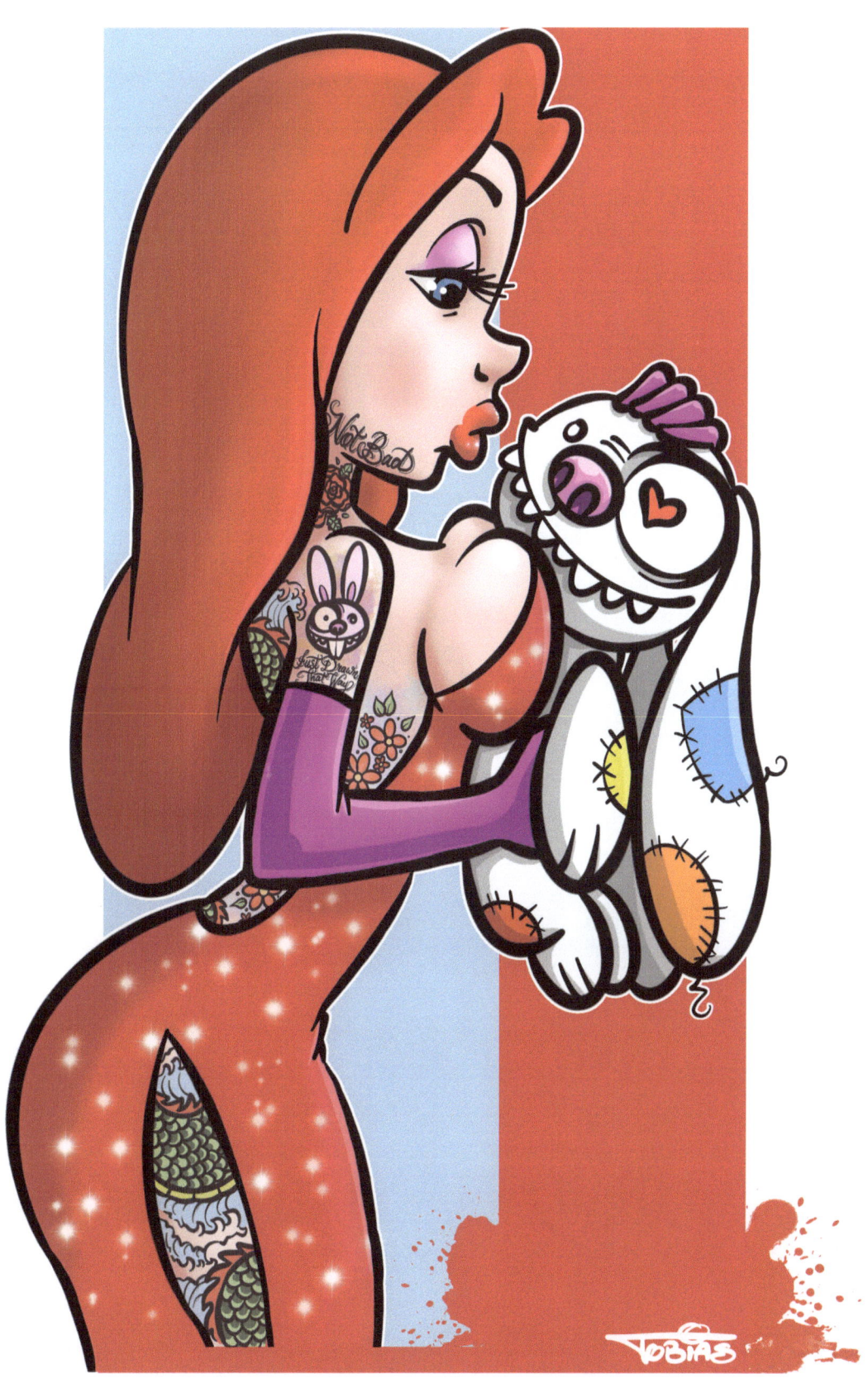

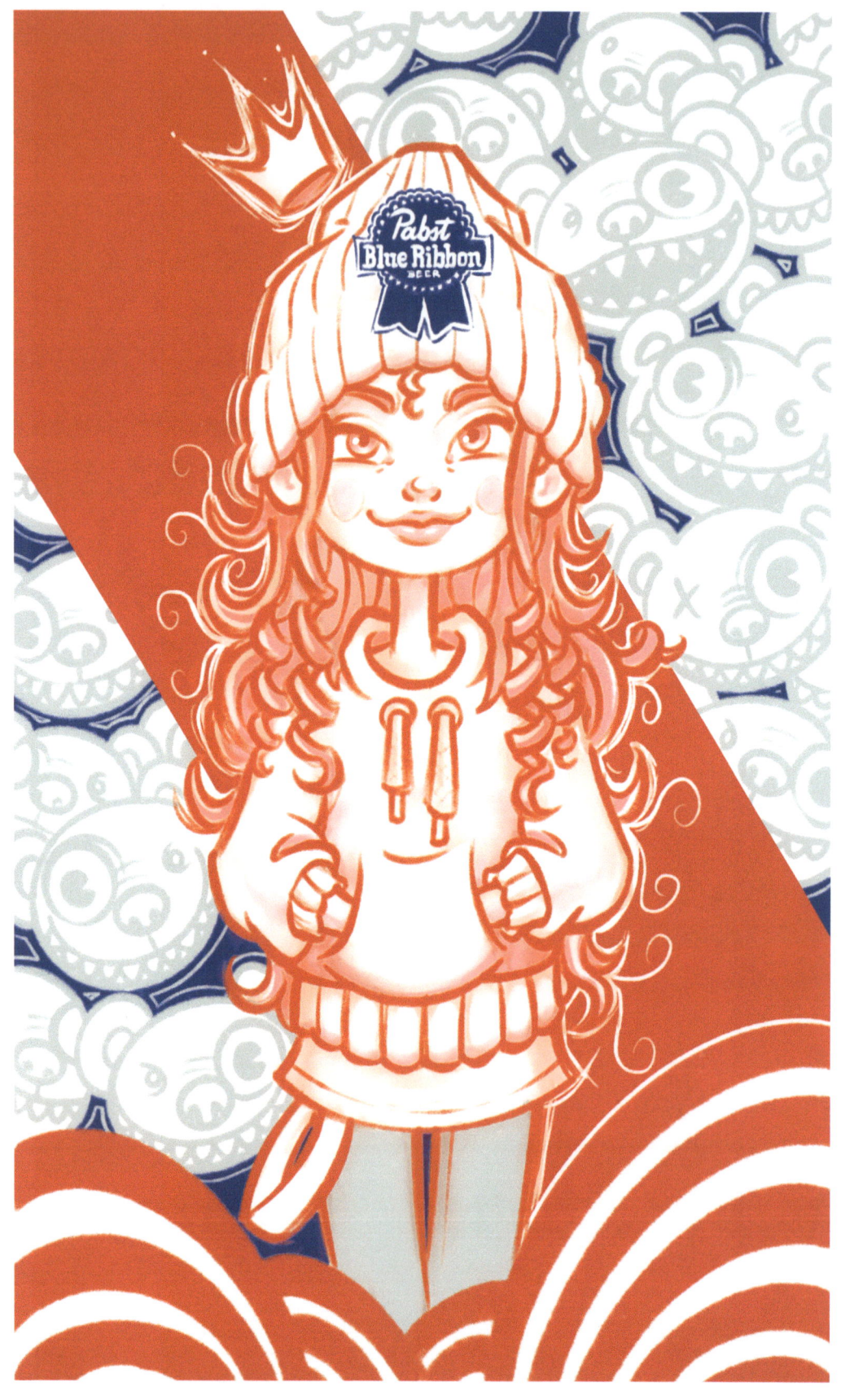

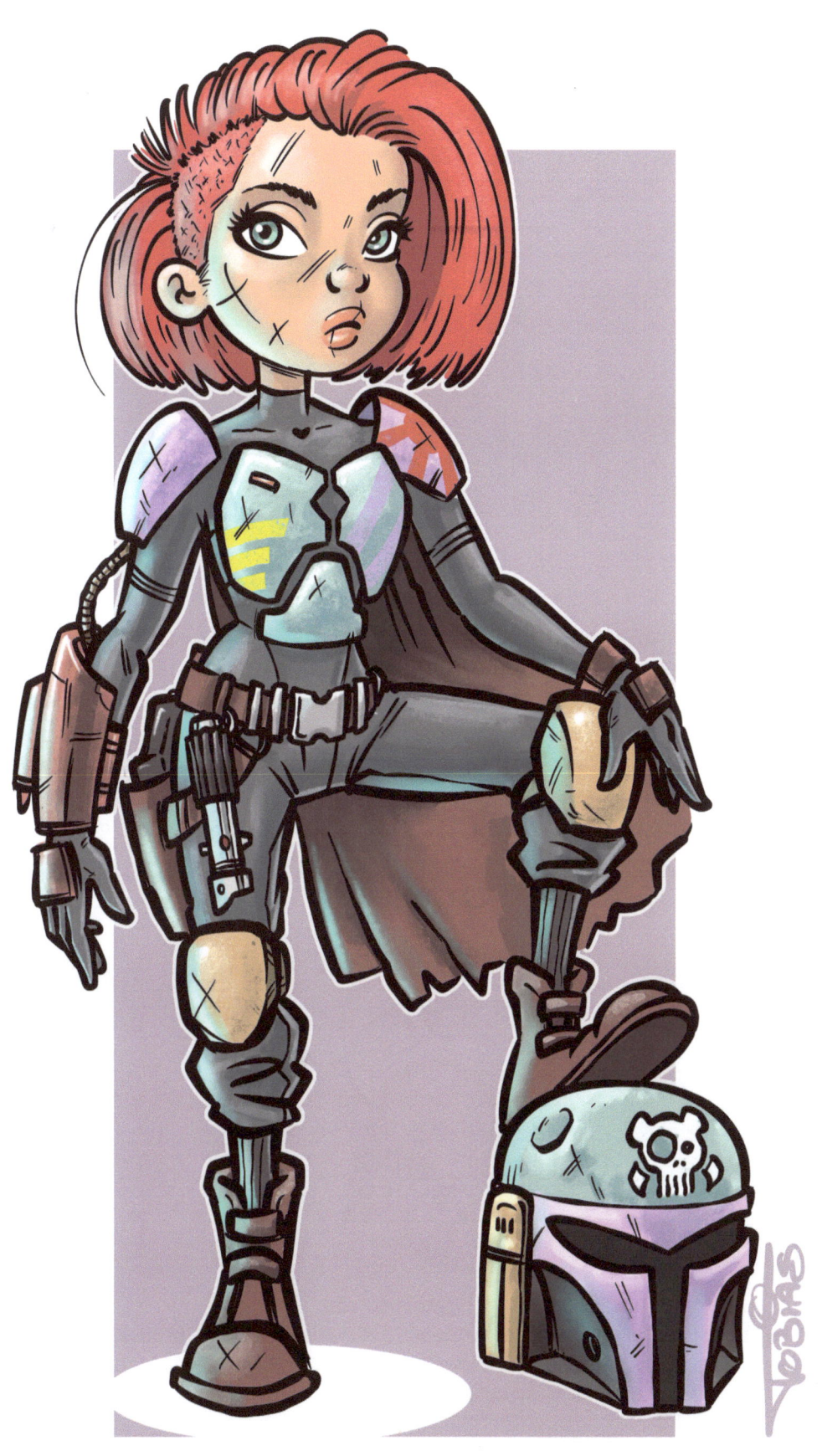

Tobias Gebhardt
Cartoonist/Illustrator

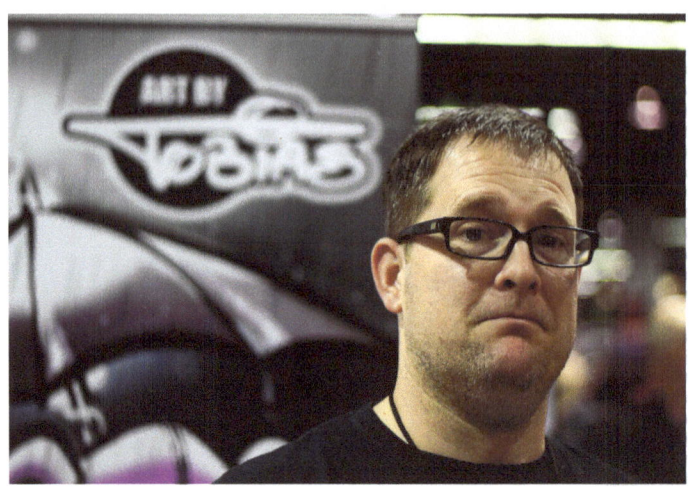

Hello There!
Thank you for aquiring this book.
As you may have noticed, it is filled with artwork.
A good decade or more of art I've created and sold at a variety of conventions and shows.
These are what I consider the best and most popular designs, along with some of my personal favorites all the way through the end of 2019.
I hope you enjoy this book as much as I enjoyed creating its content.

Best Regards,
Tobias

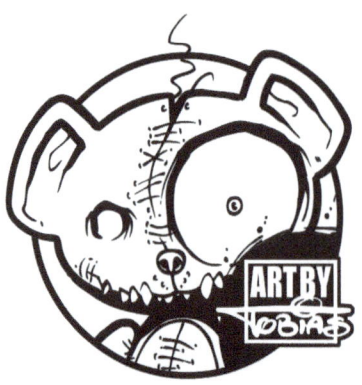

©Art By Tobias. All rights reserved.
All rights reserved. No portion of this book may be reproduced in any form without permission from the publisher, except as permitted by U.S. copyright law. For permissions contact:
info@artbytobias.com
www.artbytobias.com

www.ingramcontent.com/pod-product-compliance
Lightning Source LLC
Chambersburg PA
CBHW051208220526
45473CB00003B/945